DEDIC

This book is dedicated to the "collective" Black America. I love you.
I love you with every fiber in my being. I have researched you,
studied you and watched you for 49 years. You, collectively, can do
anything you put your mind to. You can compete with anyone, at
anything, on any level. History has recorded same. Nobody is
better than you. Nobody! But you must believe that yourself. You
have to know this deep down.

Time is of the essence. Black America it is imperative that you git
spiritually, mentally and physically fit. Create a "collective" plan and
implement "collective" strategies for its execution. Develop a
"collective" agenda and itinerary. Get your map, compass,
backpack, water, c-rations, first-aid kit, boots, can opener, hunting
knife, change of clothes and move forward.

There are no more muthaphuckin' excuses. That "poor me" victim
shit is old and played out. Don't nobody want to hear that shit.
Shut the fuck up and git to work. Put your blame-thrower down and
pick up the mirror and look at yo' self! What are you doin'
"collectively"? Where are you goin' "collectively"? Why are you
here? What about your posterity? Do you love them? If you do,
then show the world.

Whatever you "collectively" envision, conceive, imagine or desire is
within you and right in front of your face, you can have it and bring
it into physical real-world manifestation.

But you must act!

Sean Xavier Gunby, Sr.

SPECIAL DEDICATION

This book is especially dedicated to the person (a beautiful Puerto Rican Boriquen female) who put money on my books every other month or whenever I called and said I needed money while I was in The Feds. Sent me books and study materials every time I asked while I was in prison. Accepted ALL of my phone calls while I was in prison.

Helped me get on my feet when I got released from prison. Took me shopping for underwear, socks, shirts, pants, pajamas, jackets, T-shirts, food, appliances, cooking pots, frying pans, utensils, soap, car repairs, cash, **(EVERYTHING WE NEEDED)** for both me and Lil Sean.

I could not get an apartment fresh out of prison as I had no income, my credit was fucked up, I was over $900,000 in debt and couldn't pass the application credit check. She signed for me to get my apartment with her credit and her income so that me and Lil Sean would have some place to live of our own.

You have a friend FOR LIFE in me. As soon as I "git right", you gonna git all that back you gave to me and Lil Sean plus a little extra on top.

Thank you and I love you always

Sean

ABOUT THE AUTHOR

Sean Xavier Gunby, Sr. was born in Passaic, New Jersey and raised in Clifton, New Jersey. He has lived in Atlanta, Georgia, and other towns and cities in North Jersey.

Sean has a Bachelor of Science degree in Accounting from Morris Brown College *(a Historically Black College & University located in Atlanta, GA).*

Sean earned his Master of Science degree in Financial Management from the New Jersey Institute of Technology in Newark, New Jersey where he graduated Cum Laude.

Sean earned his Ph.D., Doctorate degree in The Feds at Federal Correctional Institution at Morgantown in Morgantown, West Virginia.

Sean is a professional golf caddie.

Sean has worked in the corporate world as a Financial Analyst doing mergers & acquisitions of real estate brokerage companies throughout the United States. As a Financial Analyst, Sean played a major role in the analysis and acquisition of over 100 real estate brokerage companies throughout the United States of America with an annual Sales Volume of over $10 Billion dollars.

Sean has taught as an Adjunct Professor of Pre-Algebra at Passaic County Community College in Paterson, NJ, Bergen County Community College in Paramus, NJ and Essex County College in Newark, NJ.

He was a licensed New Jersey Real Estate Broker and operated a successful realty brokerage, tax preparation and consulting business with over 1,300 clients in 17 different states until he allowed greed to infect his spirit and mind which lead to him being indicted and pleading guilty to getting his clients back bigger refunds than they were entitled to by overstating deductions and credits. These were federal charges and resulted in Sean serving 15 months, 15 days and 19 hours in The United States Federal Bureau of Prisons or "The Feds".

Sean remains an expert real estate investor.

Sean is an experienced stock and options trader and trades his own account.

Today, Sean is a published author and lives in North Jersey, owns and operates a successful window cleaning business and is a Professional Black Father of a Black Sun.

THE IMPETUS FOR WRITING THIS LITERARY DOCUMENT

This document is the follow-up and continuation of **aSTIGMAtism In My Soul – Volume I**, which was essentially my resume or introduction to the literary world. I needed Volume I to be as transparent, candid, forthright, courageous and as honest as can be in order to earn your trust and let you know that if it comes off my pen….. the shit is REAL.

With Volume II, I turn it up on Black America, the beautiful race of people to which I am a proud card-carrying member. I pull out the mirror on Black America. I take the "blame thrower" away from "us" and in turn ask us some serious questions regarding our existence. I expose and highlight that continually lamenting about the "past" and "looking backwards" is a horrible strategy and when examined intensely and closely is shown to be a mental illness.

Yes, you must know your history. Yes, you must know from whence you came. Yes, you can never forget the people that fucked you around. However, you must get the fuck up, dust yourself off and keep muthaphuckin' pushin' forward…No matter what the fuck has happened and stop fuckin' yo' self around.

"Hate" is a big expense. "Hate" is a thief. "Hate" will fuckin' stagnate and kill yo ass. This is too expensive for Black America, we cannot afford this. Yes, fucked up things have been done to us by America, but so fuckin' what. Its over. It's the past. Nobody cares. NOBODY CARES! We have to move on, turn the page, change the channel and play a new song. We have to move on!

What are we going to do TODAY, TOMORROW and NEXT WEEK. This is of utmost importance. What the fuck are we doing? Where are we going?

Hence,

aSTIGMAtism In My Soul – Volume II

A NOTE FROM THE AUTHOR

In this document, **aSTIGMAtism In My Soul – Volume II**, you will notice my exemplary grammatical skills at work. Here and now, I made a conscious decision and sustained effort, to raise the frequency and elevate my penmanship game.

Hence, I took more care and was more vigilant in my grammatical display, paragraph construction, literary structure, word play, spelling, typos, corrections, punctuations, etc.

As you continue to read my works, you will perpetually observe marked improvements in my writing texture, sentence structure, continuity of thought and overall grammatical discipline.

I will continue to turn my writing game up on y'all Niggas and rise with each project. The Phoenix flies!

Thank you

Sean Xavier Gunby, Sr.

This document was not proof-read, checked for spelling, perused for typos or edited by anyone but me. I don't need another muthaphucka to edit my shit. I'll do the footwork, I'll do the heavy lifting, I'll be the sleuth, I'll be the mistake retriever; and as long as I do my absolute best……..I'm satisfied and can look myself squarely in the eyes in the mirror and say to my soul…… Peace …. Be still.

On "Nigga"

This word has many uses, connotations, implications, designations, meanings, interpretations, variations, explanations and definitions. Some I don't even know exist and I'mma Nigga. This is a "free to use" word anywhere, anytime, in any type of setting, amongst anyone. The membership pass to use said word, is reserved for those who have inherently self-proclaimed themselves "a Nigga".

This self-proclamation transcends financial net worth, religion, socio economic status, political affiliation, creed, ethnicity or background. Anyone can self-proclaim themself a Nigga. Anyone can refer to anyone else as a Nigga in the company of anyone as long as they possess that "inner quality of Nigga self-proclamation".

How can you determine, ascertain and conclude that this someone has "membership" to freely espouse the word Nigga?

Well, in my opinion and it has been my experience, that the inflection of the voice, the pronunciation, eye contact or lack thereof, subsequent words used after uttering Nigga, demeanor and body language are critical indicators that determine "membership" in the "free to use Nigga" Nigga class. By decoding the aforementioned signals, a "Real Nigga" can ascertain whether Nigga was used in the right way, in the proper context and in the proper sound or enunciation. I would surmise that Nigga can be used in thousands, hundreds of thousands or millions of different ways depending upon the region of the world the user is in, age group, racial make-up, background, ethnicity, what he/she is describing, how, when, where and who.

I love the word Nigga. I love saying the word Nigga. I have been speaking the word for decades and plan to continue to speak it until the day I pass on to the next life. I used it yesterday, last week, last month, today, will use it tomorrow and forever. I love saying it. I speak it all the time to anyone, I don't give a fuck! I am not ashamed of saying it either because it belongs to a certain type of person from a certain type of experience and only anotha Nigga can know and appreciate how anotha Nigga says Nigga when speaking and having a conversation.

There are many uses of the word Nigga. Some are:

My Nigga, pussy ass nigga, bitch ass nigga, fly ass nigga, cool ass nigga, weak ass nigga, I don't fuck wit dat nigga, I don't fuck wit dem niggaz, fuck dem niggaz, strong ass nigga, dumb-ass nigga, stupid-ass nigga, dat nigga aight, dat nigga ain't shit, solid nigga, fag-ass nigga, gay-ass nigga, faggot-ass nigga, silly-ass nigga, smart nigga, hustlin'-ass nigga, thorough nigga, dem niggas, them niggas, too many for me to list. But the most important Nigga to be and the best nigga to be ever, in my opinion, is a **REAL NIGGA!**

++

PRESS RELEASE   *Contact:* The Universe

For Immediate Release   *999.999.999 Pineal Gland Code*

FEBRUARY 2018

THE UNIVERSE IS FED UP!! BLACK AMERICA INDICTED ON CHARGES OF UNDERPERFORMANCE, UNDERACHIEVMENT AND WEAKNESS!

The Sun, Milky Way Galaxy, The Universe – The Universe is none to pleased with the "collective" performance of BLACK AMERICA and has filed an expedited indictment to bring BLACK AMERICA before The Universal Court to answer to it's charges of under achievement, under performance and weakness.

The Universe looks upon with disdain and cares nothing for the "few" Black Americans who so call "make it" and do nothing to help the "collective" Black Americans. The Universe feels that despite BLACK AMERICA's set back, reverse or bad circumstance of physical slavery here in America (of which his cousins in Africa helped facilitate by selling them into slavery), that even given that "life experience", that BLACK AMERICA in 2018 should be further along than where it currently is.

The Universe has filed ethereally organic vibrations and frequencies to expedite the trial.

###

INDICTMENT

SUN, MOON & STARS, UNIVERSAL COURT
DISTRICT OF BLACK AMERICA

THE UNIVERSE	:	Spiritual No. 9
	:	
	:	The Cosmos
v.	:	
	:	
	:	
BLACK AMERICA	:	INDICTMENT

The Supreme Jury in and for the Sun, Moon &
Stars, Universe Court, sitting at Black America, charges:

COUNTS

1. At all times relevant to this indictment,
    defendant BLACK AMERICA, was a resident of
    The Universe under The Sun, Moon & Stars,
    and was endowed by The Universe to be Man
    and Woman in accord and in sync with The
    Universe.

2. To date, defendant BLACK AMERICA has been,
    by choice, under its own volition, ineffective,
    disorganized, fragmented and useless.

3. BLACK AMERICA has by choice, under its own
    volition, relegated itself to be the court jesters
    and buffoons of the world. It prides itself on
    telling jokes, dancing, singing, coonin' and
    performing in arenas via athletics.

4. To date, defendant BLACK AMERICA resides in
    the United States of America *(the wealthiest
    nation on Earth with nominal GDP of $18.46
    Trillion),* Black America has a spending power
    of approximately **$1.3 Trillion US Dollars** in
    and of itself yet BLACK AMERICA does not even
    produce a pair of drawers, panties, brassier,
    sanitary napkin, tooth brush, tooth paste for
    itself. This $1.3 Trillion spending power makes
    BLACK AMERICA the 12th richest nation on
    Earth ahead of Russia, Australia and Spain.

5. To date, BLACK AMERICA is looked upon by other member nations of the world as pieces of shit, a waste, stupid, idiots, children of a lesser God, buffoons, clowns. This viewpoint is made manifest and valid, confirmed and supported by BLACK AMERICA through its own behavior.

6. To date, BLACK AMERICA still looks at its former slave master as it's "Daddy" and expects and demands that it's "Daddy" continue to take care of it and provide for it. BLACK AMERICA has refused to grow up and take its position on the world stage and become a responsible and productive member of The Universe.

7. To date, BLACK AMERICA has allowed itself to become weak, lethargic, sedentary, listless, useless, co-dependent and pussyfied. BLACKAMERICA is in last place on the world stage. BLACK AMERICA has no map, compass, itinerary, agenda, leadership, water, rations, food, direction, aim or strategy. It's just going through life "hoping the lawd" will come to its rescue. Currently, Donald Trump is the leader of BLACK AMERICA as BLACK AMERICA has no leader.

8. To date, BLACK AMERICA is a co-author in destroying itself. BLACK AMERICA hates himself/herself. It suffers from serious and grave mental illnesses and disorders stemming from its past physical captivity or slavery. It uses this as an excuse for its substandard performance and under achievement.

9. To date, BLACK AMERICA, more specifically, the BLACK AMERICAN MALE has failed his family in most cases, not all. He does not provide any real meaningful leadership to his posterity. He has allowed himself to be anesthetized with smokin' weed, money, sneakers, the BMW, the Rolex, diamonds, pussy, thereby effectively saying "fuck you" to his own posterity.

10. To date, BLACK AMERICA has refused to clean up its own neighborhoods. In every major city in the USA, wherever BLACK AMERICA is, is the most fucked up part of town. BLACK AMERICA has shirked its responsibility to provide a safe learning ground for its posterity.

11. BLACK AMERICA does not love its posterity as it makes no preparations, plans and leaves no provisions for the youth to build upon. BLACK AMERICA has effectively abandoned it's post and committed treason to its own-self.

It is the mandate of the Court of The Sun, Moon and Stars that BLACK AMERICA having been duly indicted that we proceed to the Jury Trial phase of this case.

It is the feeling of the Court that "time being of the essence" the Court is mandating that all parties move expeditiously, quickly and with haste to prepare for the Jury Trial, as the Court will not wait another nanosecond for BLACK AMERICA to get its defense argument prepared.

Jury Trial is set to begin immediately. Please begin Jury selection.

THE REST OF THIS PAGE INTENTIONALLY LEFT BLANK

THE UNIVERSE CHOOSES JURY MEMBERS

The Universe has chosen its jury in the case against Black America. The Universe has chosen both Male and Female jurors to decide the case. The Jury members for The Universe are listed below:

Muhammad Ali, Chairman
Malcolm X
Fred Hampton
Huey P. Newton
Lewis Latimer
Benjamin Banneker
Garrett Morgan
James Brown
Martin Luther King, Jr.
Adam Clayton Powell
Michael Jackson
Elijah McCoy
Granville Woods
Jesse Owens
Morris Brown
Richard Pryor
Curtis Mayfield
Ivan Van Sertima
Vivien Theodore Thomas
Daniel Hale Williams
Dr. Charles Drew
Eazy Muthaphuckin' E
Professor X
Nat Turner

Rosa Parks
Madame C.J. Walker
Esther Rolle
Fannie Lou Hamer
Harriet Tubman
Mary McLeod Bethune
Shirley Chisolm
Althea Gibson
Wilma Rudolph
Katherine Coleman Goble Johnson
Mary Jackson
Dorothy Johnson Vaughn

SENTENCING

SUN, MOON & STARS, UNIVERSAL COURT
DISTRICT OF BLACK AMERICA

THE UNIVERSE   :   Spiritual No. 9
                :
                :   The Cosmos
    v.   :
                :
                :
BLACK AMERICA   :   <u>INDICTMENT</u>

We the Jury of The Universe, Sun, Moon and Stars find the
defendant, BLACK AMERICA, guilty on all counts. We the jury, find
BLACK AMERICA weak, effeminate, ineffectual, dazed, confused,
disorganized, pussyfied, lost, distracted, aimless, directionless, a
hater of itself, a hater of its posterity, co-dependent of white
America, a habitual welfare recipient, a shirker of responsibility,
unengaged, no enthusiasm, listless, broken down spiritually,
mentally and physically, physically over-weight and obese, on
medications that can be cured with proper diet and exercise, a
mis-manager of its funds, financially illiterate, addicted to
electronic devices.

There are no more excuses BLACK AMERICA for your under-
performance.

GUILTY! GUILTY! GUILTY! GUILTY!

Commentary from members of the jury:

Muhammad Ali, Chairman of the Jury
Black American Male, I showed you what your "will" and
"confidence" can achieve. I showed you that money was nothing
and gave it all up to stand up for principle and what is right. And
by doing so, I got it all back 50-fold. I taught you "love of self"
and that "Black is Beautiful". I showed you resiliency,
perseverance and how to "comeback". You didn't hear a word that
I said. I am ashamed and embarrassed of you. I find you
GUILTY!

Madame CJ Walker

Black American Female, I was born in 1867 in Louisiana during the 19th century. I showed you what your "will" and "confidence" can achieve. I showed you discipline and focus and that anything can be achieved if you put your mind to it. I was the first female millionaire, Black or white, in America. Here it is the 21st century and you chose mediocrity, section 8, welfare and public assistance over "trying"? I am ashamed and embarrassed of you. I find you GUILTY!

Garrett Morgan

Black American Male, I was born in 1877 in Kentucky during the 19th Century. I invented the gas mask and the traffic signal. What are you doing? What do you manufacture? What do you make that you sell to the world? What's wrong with you? It's the 21st century. I am ashamed and embarrassed of you. I find you GUILTY!

Huey P. Newton

Black American Male, I showed you that you have to protect your Black family, children and community from anybody, even stupid ass niggas. I showed you the power of organization, study and knowing the law. What are you doing Black Man? You are not acting like men. I am ashamed and embarrassed of you. I find you GUILTY!

Katherine Coleman Goble Johnson, Mary Jackson, Dorothy Johnson Vaughn

Black American Female, we showed you that computers weren't necessary and that "by hand" we could do the mathematics to send NASA spaceships up into space. That's being "precise", "accurate", "determined" and "focused". We showed you how to "use your brains". We had supreme confidence in everything we did. What has happened to you in 2018? What are you doing? We are ashamed and embarrassed of you. We find you GUILTY!

Althea Gibson

Black American Female, I was born in South Carolina in 1927, moved to Harlem and became the 1st Black athlete to win a Grand Slam in professional tennis. I showed you COURAGE, DEDICATION, CONCENTRATION and STRENGTH. What are you doing? Where are you going? I am ashamed and embarrassed of you I find you GUILTY!

Lewis Latimer
Black American Male, I showed you what your "mind power" and "dedication" can achieve. I improved on Thomas Edison's lightbulb which he could only keep lit for a few hours. I invented the carbon filament in the light bulb that allowed it to stay lit for weeks and months. I lit up the world. What's wrong with you? Do you have a plan? I am ashamed and embarrassed of you. I find you GUILTY!

Benjamin Banneker
Black American Male, I showed you what your "mind and research" can achieve. I had no formal education and was "SELF TAUGHT". I wrote the first almanac in America and made the 1st clock in 1753 during the 18th century. I was an astronomer. I don't understand what's wrong with you? Do you have a plan? I am ashamed and embarrassed of you. I find you GUILTY!

Michael Jackson
Black American Male, I showed you to strive for perfection, work ethic and business acumen. I had 1 album that sold over 104 million copies (a world record to this day). I gave away over $250 Million to charity. My music videos are so perfect that no artist today in 2018 can top the Thriller, Beat it or Billie Jean videos. That's "dedication to perfection". You have to do better than what you are doing. I am ashamed and embarrassed of you. I find you GUILTY!

Wilma Rudolph
Black American Female, I was born in Jim Crow Tennessee a very sickly child with pneumonia, scarlet fever and infantile paralysis caused by polio and wore a leg brace until I was 8 yrs. old. I shrugged that off, "raised my vibration" and became a World Record holding Olympic Champion sprinter. I was declared the fastest woman in the world in the 1960's. Where is your "fight"? "determination"? I am ashamed and embarrassed of you. I find you GUILTY!

James Brown
Black American Male, You know me. I loved you. I was inducted into the Rock N Roll Hall of Fame the 1st year it opened. **I am Soul Brutha #1.** I told you to "Say It Loud I'm Black and I'm Proud" in 1968. I told the world that Black is Beautiful and always kept my Black American style, walk, talk, dress and attitude in-tact. 50 years later it seems like some of y'all don't want to be Black no more? What's up? You abandoning your families? Are you a quitter Black Man?. I am ashamed and embarrassed of you. I find you GUILTY!

Esther Rolle

Black American Female, I played Florida Evans on Good Times in the 1970's. I gained my fame late in my life because I refused to take demeaning, coonin' and buffoonery roles in Hollywood. I fought hard for the "father figure" character on Good Times and rebelled and spoke out against JJ's coonin' and buffoonery. I eventually left the show because I refused to participate in the display of Black people acting like clowns and jesters. What's up? Where is your Black American Pride? I am ashamed and embarrassed of you. I find you GUILTY!

Richard Pryor

Black American Male, You know me. I taught you honesty, forthrightness and that we should love being Niggas. Everybody on the planet wants to be like Niggas but Niggas. I made you laugh but there was always some Black Power shit behind what I was saying. Be proud Niggas. Don't be ashamed and run from your Nigganess...that your strength! Keep it Real! Speak up! Say what it is Black Man! I am ashamed and embarrassed of you. I find you GUILTY!

Eazy Muthaphuckin' E

Black American Male from the late 1980's. You know me. I brought you that West Coast "gangsta shit". Wouldn't be no Ice Cube or Dr. Dre without me. I put dem Niggas on. I taught you entrepreneurship, ownership, concentration, planning and execution. I spoke out and said what the fuck it was. What are y'all doing in 2018? West Coast Niggas y'all need to "Stand Up". I am ashamed and embarrassed of you. I find you GUILTY!

Malcolm X

Black American Male, I showed you and told you to "do for self", "stop begging white America to help you with things you can do for yourself", "look in the mirror and help yourself". I told you these things 57 years ago and they've proven prophetic. Look at you!! Look at you in 2018! You are in disarray, disorganized and you are a wreck! You have chosen material wealth over your dignity, honor, integrity, children, family, yourself and your Black American swagger. I am hurt to my heart. Did I waste my time? I am ashamed and embarrassed of you. I find you GUILTY!

On Kobe vs. Jordan

I'm 48 years old as of the writing of this brief soliloquy of what "I saw" as it relates to this topic, In my opinion. I've heard this topic discussed in Black barbershops throughout the USA, at Black family reunions and we used to discuss it at length on the yard or in the Unit in federal prison (debates used to get heated).

It has been my experience that Jordan is most often selected and cited as the better than Kobe and consequently the best ever to play the game. His 6 rings is almost always uniformly screamed as the measuring stick, ruler or scale as to why he is better than Kobe. His MVP's, finals MVP's, scoring titles, etc. are next to be spoken of to support the Jordan argument.

I saw both Niggaz play their entire careers (not YouTube clips of highlights and shit) and Jordan was a BAD MUTHAPHUCKA and in my opinion, he did play in a tougher era when the NBA was 6x more physical than it was during Kobe's era. Jordan is one of the greatest to ever do it in my opinion.

Deservedly so, Jordan was the face of the NBA and was a "marketing juggernaut" for the NBA, Nike, Gatorade, Hanes, etc., so given all of this monetary investment by corporate America, it was in everybody's interest to "pump, re-pump and continue to pump" Jordan during his career and even after his career as they do now because there is still significant investment dollars on the table. But I reiterate, the accolades that Jordan got and still gets is meritorious, earned, deserved and rightfully bestowed upon him. I must repeat this. Jordan, after Dr. J (Converse), had a real "mega sneaker deal" which catapulted him even further into the stratosphere from a marketing perspective.

Kobe fucked his chance up, or somebody fucked Kobe's chance up, to be the next "marketing juggernaut" of the NBA, when he was accused and indicted for raping that white girl. This fucked his marketing shit up and excluded him from being the "face of the NBA", in my opinion. But this did not deter him nor make him "go against himself" and quit. It seemed to motivate and drive him to say "I'mma show you muthaphuckas what the fuck this shit is" and in hindsight he did just that and overcame that small blemish to where now nobody even talks about that shit when discussing Kobe.

I say all of the aforementioned things to lay the groundwork and add some color to my position on this topic of **"Kobe vs. Jordan"**. I think I am justified in doing same as the media has the ability to "build or destroy" weak minds perception of people, situation, events, etc. It takes a real strong, penetrating and discerning mind to get to the root of some shit. I possess one of these minds.

In my opinion, Kobe is the baddest Nigga to ever lace up a pair of gym sneakers and pick up a basketball. In my muthaphuckin' opinion!

Scottie Pippen (Hall of Famer) has 6 rings and was voted one of the 50 Greatest Ever to play in the NBA. Dennis Rodman (Hall of Famer) is arguably the greatest rebounder in the history of the NBA. Jordan had these Niggaz on his team. I can't discount this. In my opinion, without these 2 niggaz Jordan don't get 6 rings. Now proponents and supporters of Jordan are gonna scream at the top of their lungs "KOBE HAD SHAQ!!! SHAQ!!". This is true. But Shaq had Kobe too. They only won 3 rings together. Kobe has 5. His last 2 rings that he won he won with a rag-tag, Kmart team. Not dissing those players but they were not Scottie Pippen or Dennis Rodman level players. They were good role players that played their parts well.

In my opinion,

- Kobe had a better jump shot than Jordan;
- Kobe shot the 3 better than Jordan;
- With 11 seconds left on the clock, no timeouts and you down by 1, Kobe was a better closer, killer;
- Defense I give a slight edge to Jordan, but oh so slight;
- Athleticism is a tie;
- Post-up game is a tie even though Kobe bit Jordan's whole style and game; (but shit anybody can copy Jordan but if you don't make the shots it don't mean shit);
- Kobe won more with less talent on his team than Jordan;
- "In game" high flying, acrobatic shit, dunks I give to Kobe;

I'm fuckin' wit Kobe! Fuck it!

P.S. Neither Jordan nor Kobe could match the "Soul, Gallantry, Artistry, Smoothness, Gracefulness, Awe, In air visual effects, Black Power Nigganess on the basketball court, leaping ability, take flight with body part theatrics that made a muthaphucka say "Man did you see that shit" like Dr. J.

You can watch Dr. J highlights today in 2018 that he did 45 years ago that make Jordan and Kobe look like little bitty children. Nigga had that Big Beautiful Black Power Afro that used to blow in the wind when that Nigga took off soaring toward the bucket. Dr. J would take off first and come down last. Nigga had a swagger unseen then and since on a basketball court.

Let's get this shit right. Y'all Niggas say Kobe bit off Jordan (which he did in my opinion) but Jordan got his shit from "The Dr." point blank and frank.

Peace out Niggaz!

Oh yeah, I almost forgot.

Larry Bird is the baddest white boy to every do it. I hated this nigga back in the 80's and the muthaphuckin' Celtics. But at 48 years old, in hindsight, looking back, this white boy was a BAD MUTHAPHUCKA!!! When he got the ball you knew most of time that shit was going in. He was Nasty on the court and dead muthaphuckin' serious and didn't take no shit. And he played against some MONSTERS during his era and never shrunk from a challenge.

Muthaphucka could flat our shoot! Played D, could pass, and was a World Champion and carried a franchise for years on his back. Under pressure was nothing for him. He didn't give a fuck he was gonna find a way to win and usually did.

If I got 12 seconds left on the clock, no timeouts and I'm down by a basket there is only 1 player (Kobe) that I would run my play through before Larry Bird. NOBODY ELSE in the history of the game would I run my play through before Larry Bird. If it's anybody else other than Kobe, and I may make Kobe stand down, I'm telling them "GIVE THE BALL TO LARRY BIRD AND GET THE FUCK OUT THE WAY"....

I'm gone!

On Professor PLO Lumumba

About 6 weeks ago a friend of mine turned me on to this dude via a YouTube video and since viewing that very first video I've been inspired, attentive and have become a fan of this man. I fucks wit PLO Lumumba. This dude is a real man's man. He cuts no corners and sugar coats nothing of what he says regarding his topic which most often is "corruption in Africa" and "the continent of Africa punching below its weight".

I love that. I love that he don't give a fuck who likes or dislikes what he says. He says it anyway. I can see and feel his conviction when he speaks. He is articulate and enunciates his words with perfection. His diction is proper, eloquent and to the point. I love this. He loves Africa as he describes himself as a "Pan Africanist". He believes in Africa. He breathes Africa. He tells Africans what they do not want to hear but NEED to hear. He speaks to his fellow Africans about very uncomfortable topics and issues and does not put a big red bow on it. He gives it to them raw. I love this.

To me, in my opinion, Professor PLO Lumumba is a man.

And I don't mean a man in the gender sense, that he has a penis and nuts, because there are plenty of these types that are really female in spirit, heart and mind. But a man in the sense that he is masculine in his energy, vibration, speak and delivery.

PLO Lumumba is taking the leaders/leadership of various, many and all of the 56 African nations to task and telling them in a more eloquent and politically correct way than I will to "stop acting like fuckin' snake muthaphuckas" and selling out your own people for money and personal selfish gain. He goes into great detail about countries like the Democratic Republic of Congo that is the "richest resource rich country on the continent of Africa" with over $3 or $34 Trillion US Dollars of "rare earth" under its belly. Yet the Congo stays in constant civil conflict and turmoil with Congolese killing Congolese.

Maybe Black Americans should consider exporting their intellectual capital to The Congo and helping the Congolese "git right" and in the same breath, create generational wealth for their own individual families by getting in at the ground floor.

He mentions Nigeria, a very oil rich nation, that doesn't control any of its oil. Angola, Somalia, Kenya, Rwanda, Mozambique, Swaziland, all of them he touches upon as not living up to their real and true potential. That the leaders/leadership are all on the take from Western, Chinese and European powers and that it is this corruption that is holding Africa back.

He touches upon individual African countries and that the native African wants and strives to be like their former colonizer instead of being themselves. That if a country was colonized by France, the Africans there today strive to be French instead of Senegalese. If a country was colonized by Britain, then todays Africans in that respective country strive to behave as the British do and talk like them as opposed to being themselves.

As a Black American who has travelled to Africa several times, I found this quite shocking because a lot of times when I see Africans here in the United States they sometimes act as if they don't want to fuck with us or they are somehow superior to Black Americans and can look down on Black Americans with condescension (in some cases NOT ALL). And here it is that they are just as fucked up, if not more, than Black Americans are.

The history of slavery in America, 500+ years ago, according to history, myth or folklore, is that certain African kings captured and sold rival tribes into slavery as a result of inter-tribal warfare (Africans sold Africans into slavery... in other words we fucked ourselves). Now here it is in 2018, the African leadership is doing the self-same thing with the natural resources, minerals and assets today, selling their own people, nations and continent into slavery so they, the individual leaders, can have apartments in London, NYC, Dubai, Paris, etc.

Shit is demoralizing.

As Professor PLO Lumumba would ask: "Are Blacks/Africans children of a lesser God?"

What is Africa's agenda? Does Africa have an agenda? Does Africa have an itinerary? Does Africa have a map? Does Africa have a compass? Does Africa have a plan?

Or

Is their plan, agenda and itinerary to continue to be "under achievers", **never missing an opportunity to miss an opportunity**, to continue to be the "scar on the planet Earth", to continue to sit at the white man's feet and beg for help and crumbs from the table.

PLO Lumumba says there are 3 ways to be at the banquet:

1. As a diner
2. As a waiter
3. As food to be eaten

"Choose you now"...   Which will you be?

Left up to the sucka-ass, faggot-ass, greedy ass, stupid ass, weak ass, miseducated ass African leaders/leadership.... Africa will remain option #3.

Fuckin' stupid muthaphuckas! Weak muthaphuckas.

How the fuck you gonna be the largest Continent on the planet Earth, blessed with the most natural resources, minerals, oil, natural gas, most different species of plants, fish, animals, birds, endless water supply, continuous Sun solar power, 1.3 Billion population and you are in last muthaphuckin' place?

Viet Nam was damn near burned to the ground just 50 years ago as a result of a civil war and today has a burgeoning growing economy. Japan was fuckin' burned to the ground 73 years ago (Hiroshima, Nagasaki) and today is the #1 automobile producer on the planet (Toyota, Honda, Nissan, Acura, Infiniti, Lexus, Subaru). China just gained its independence from Japan 69 years ago and today has a $11 Trillion economy, manufacturing damn near any and everything.

What is wrong with you African muthaphuckas? Stop fuckin' fighting each other and "Get Right" and come up. Stand up and be a man.

The youth of Africa must not tolerate nor continue to accept crooked ass, under-performing leaders/leadership regardless of ethnic extraction and must demand (through blood shed if necessary) that anyone entrusted with a leadership position who chooses to misuse and abuse that position for personal gain, to the detriment of the unborn African posterity, will be dealt with swiftly, harshly and decisively with their lives. Once this precedent is established, Mother Africa will be on her way to "standing up" and being a diner at the banquet.

There are no excuses.

Peace out!

On Hollywood Sexual Perversion Revelations

It seems as though the lid has been lifted off of the morality jar of Hollywood, California USA, exposing it's decades of sexual perversion, homosexuality, pedophilia, rape, child molestation and flat out moral decadence infecting that society of media professionals. Recently, we have seen and heard many participants in that chosen profession of actors, actresses, directors, producers, studio executives, etc., talk of the pervasive, morally corrupt value system entrenched in lascivious and licentious behaviors that permeates Hollywood, USA.

Studio heads using the mighty leverage of "money and fame" to get "success thirsty" women and men to perform sexual favors to get a part in a movie. Executive producers using the powerful hammer of threat of "being black-balled" and never working in Hollywood again if you don't "do this or let me do that".

These are the very "super-rich" supposedly "elite", people with mayors, governors, representatives, prosecutors, judges and senators in their cell phone contacts app and have made significant campaign contributions to these self-same people so they feel (and maybe have earned through money) as though they have some extra length on their leash as it relates to their conduct and behavior.

In America most people (not all) respect a person "with money" irrespective of how he/she got it or their current behavior with it. All we say is "they got money".

In my opinion, So fuckin' what!! Big deal! Look at how these muthaphucka's are acting. Mentally abusing people, young adults and children. Abusing their power for selfish ends.

It is not lost on me that at one time in my own life and I have heard many, many other people talk about how they aspired to "go to Hollywood" to become an actor/actress and become rich and famous. How some of us looked up to, held in high esteem and tried to emulate these larger than life personalities we saw on the TV screen or in the movie theatre.

Media, whether it be TV, print or radio (what we see, hear and read) is SUPER powerful to non-discerning impressionable minds. Naïve followers, children, teenagers and young adults and shit even adults are easy prey and fall victim to these images witnessed on the TV screen in our private residences every night. The media has the power to "sway and direct" society's mind and perceptions in any way it sees fit.

Now I can understand and see why that over the past 25 years there has been an explosion of "gay homosexuality lesbian transgender" shit on TV sitcoms, commercials, cartoons, movies, music, etc. Look at the moral thought process, condition and sexual behaviors of the "people in power" in Hollywood USA. These people have the power to control what we see, hear and read on a daily basis.

In the 1970's and 1980's, you didn't see this fuckin' bombardment of sexually perverse images on the TV screen. As a matter of fact, it was more pervasive and prevalent among men, young adults and boys in society, that you didn't want to be a faggot, gay or a sissy. Then all of sudden it became "chic and en vogue" to be gay. What the fuck happened?

One of the main things that stayed pressing on my mind when I was in prison was to stay out of trouble and hurry up and get out of that bitch and get back to raising Lil Sean. With so many Black fathers in prison or missing from the household, these little Black boys are being raised by women, constantly around women, picking up the mannerisms of women, becoming emotional like women, responding to life like women, thinking like women, behaving like women and then they turn on the TV and see all this gay homosexual transgender shit and they say "it's on TV so I guess it's ok".

In my opinion, that's why the Black Father is so important to the Black American Nation, because he needs to be there to "straighten that shit" and let these little Black boys know ... "NAH MAN... that ain't how this shit go" "You a Nigga... so don't be hanging around a bunch of bitches all the time..."

Hang around other Niggas and do Nigga shit.. As a matter of fact, you gonna hang out with me and we are gonna do Nigga shit... play catch, wrestle, shadow box, tackle football, basketball, push-ups, dips, talk about masculine shit, look a muthaphucka in the eye when you talk to them, put the cell phone down, put the iPad down, put the video game down and go outside and play with the other little boys in the neighborhood."

I went to Kruger National Park in South Africa and saw all types and species of animals and never saw 2 male species fuckin' around with each other. The males were always fighting over who was going to control the females. I've watched National Geographic, Wild Kingdom and other animal channels and never saw 2 male species of anything fuckin' with each other on some sexual shit. They always trying to fuck the females. This also applies to birds in the sky, fish/marine life in the sea and mammals on land.

So why the fuck is it that the animals, birds, fish have it right and humans don't?

I know many people, men and women, even family members who are openly gay and I'm "aight" with them from a distance and I allow them to be themselves and I mind my business. I speak and say what's up but I don't hang out with them. I don't chill with dudes now but you'll never see me chillin' with a gay dude.

I am hypocritical though. I am conflicted and contradict myself. As I don't frown upon gay women with as much disdain as I do gay men. I think my reasoning is that I cherish the thought of joining 2 women and doing a 3some as I've never done one before. And it just don't seem as wrong for women as women are feminine by nature. However, for a masculine species to be feminine just looks all the way fucked up.

Fuck it! That's how I feel about it.

January 4, 2017

If you want a particular outcome in your life... it is incumbent upon you to push to bring that into existence – whatever it may be. Anything can be achieved – but you have to push through the fear.

I am 17 days short of being off Federal Supervised Release. It's almost like awaiting another re-birth. I will be totally done with my federal case. I'm excited.

I am full throttle no let up into my custody case for My Sun. How can I stand idly by and let his mother, her brother and her sister-in-law dictate my time and "my right" to father my own child? I am going to let another human being monopolize the nurturing of my own son? They are going to raise him during his formative years? Hell no! I am willing to die if need be to raise My Sun the way I see fit. I would be less than a man to take any other course of action. It's my turn!

Thursday, January 5, 2017

Whatever you desire to become, have or do in this lifetime will take the utmost commitment. Being concerned with what the next person says or thinks about what you are doing will lead you to failure. Fuck what they think? Go! Go after your vision. Go all out – throwing caution to the wind. Be scared. Be afraid. Be unsure. Be insecure. Be concerned and do the shit any muthaphuckin' way! It's the only way to live.

Today was another awesome day! I performed amazingly well as I always do.

Monday, January 9, 2017

Stop making excuses for your substandard performance in life. Trying to explain why you ain't shit. Explaining and making excuses why you are "stuck like chuck". It's cause you are a fuckin' coward – a pussy – and afraid to change, afraid to risk it all, afraid to lose, afraid to fail, afraid to be different, afraid to be criticized, afraid of what other people (who ain't shit either) are gonna say. This is why you ain't gonna be shit!!

Too cold today to do windows. 3 degrees. Tomorrow and the rest of the week it's going to be 40 degrees and higher. Will get money then. Worked out 2x today. Worked on my custody case and my bankruptcy. Very productive day.

Sunday, January 15, 2017

I have no problem and experience no psychological discomfort whatsoever when I stand on my beliefs, even if I must stand alone. I stand on my square and I do not waver one iota. Not even a fraction. I am a man first! I'mma man first!.

No matter what happens I will always be me! I don't need acceptance or approval from anyone. I stand on my own square. I will succeed. I will make it. In the end I will still be me. I will be able to live with myself and look the world squarely in the eye! I love me! I love you Sean X. Gunby, Sr.

There will be a time where it will be just "you and your faith in yourself".

When I was at FCI Morgantown another Brutha told me …

"Yes we have to believe and have faith in God – but we also must have just as much and more of the same belief and faith in that person in the mirror because we can "see" that person in the mirror but we can't see God."

Tuesday, January 17, 2017

You must always press forward in spite of doubt, fear and the unknown. If you are "Right" and you know you are "Right" then there is nothing to fear except you punkin' out. Life will be what you "will it" to be and make it to be. Nobody should be able to stop you. Make sure your game is tight and shit is "together and in order".

What I speak of is the mind and the spirit. If those 2 are clean and in harmony – anything is possible. Nothing will be impossible. You then have to couple these with discipline, concentration, dedication and determination. Quiet the mind and you quiet your soul. Visualize what it is that you want. See it in your head first. See it. See yourself there already. That is the most important piece. You have to see it. Then doing it is a piece of cake.

Actually, once you see it – it's already done!

Be True! Be Bold! Be Aggressive!

The Phoenix

A legendary bird which according to one account lived 500 years, burned itself to ashes on a pyre, and rose alive from the ashes to live another period.

Resurgence – a rising again into life, activity or prominence

Resurrect – to raise from the dead – to bring to view, attention or use again

Resurrection – to rise again – a spiritualization of thought material belief that yields to spiritual understanding

A legendary bird represented by the Ancient Egyptians as living 5 or 6 centuries in the Arabian desert, being consumed in fire by its own act, and rising in youthful freshness from its own ashes and often regarded as an emblem of immortality or of the resurrection

A person or thing likened to The Phoenix
1. A paragon of excellence or beauty
2. One that experiences a restoration, renewal or seeming re-birth after ruin or destruction

Smoke This, Sniff This, Shoot This, Drink This!

1. His opinion of me is not my reality
2. America's opinion of me is not my reality
3. Her opinion of me is not my reality
4. They opinion of me is not my reality
5. Their opinion of me is not my reality
6. **What the fuck I think of me is my reality!**

Dr. King Speech - "Where Do We Go From Here"

"To offset this cultural homicide, the Negro must rise up with an affirmation of his own Olympian manhood. Any movement for the Negro's freedom that overlooks this necessity is only waiting to be buried. As long as the mind is enslaved, the body can never be free. Psychological freedom, a firm sense of self-esteem, is the most powerful weapon against the long night of physical slavery.

No Lincolnian Emancipation Proclamation, no Johnsonian Civil Rights Bill can totally bring this kind of freedom. The Negro will only be free when he reaches down to the inner depths of his own being and signs with the pen and ink of self-assertive manhood his own emancipation proclamation. And with a spirit straining toward true self-esteem, the Negro must boldly throw off the manacles of self-abnegation and say to himself and to the world, "I Am Somebody" I am a person. I am a man with dignity and honor. I have a rich and noble history, however painful and exploited that history has been. Yes, I was a slave through my fore parents, and now I'm not ashamed of that.

Yes we must stand up and say "I'm Black, but I'm Black and Beautiful." This self-affirmation is the Black Mans need made compelling by the white man's crimes against him."

The aforementioned speech is the work of Dr. Martin Luther King, Jr., a hero of mine. A very brave and courageous man.

On Failure

Failure is a beautiful thing. Failure is the best University on the Planet Earth. It's the most advanced degree an individual can earn. It's the most enlightened and intelligent Professor in history and there is no better vessel or purveyor of knowledge. Failure sole intent is to "Git You "Right". Failure hurts. Failure torments. Failure is painful like a muthaphucka. Failure lasts until you defeat it. Failure ain't going nowhere until you whoop it's ass! The faster you run from Failure the faster Failure chases after you. The faster you step toward Failure and engage Failure, the faster Failure weakens and dies.

I don't run from Failure, I embrace Failure. For I know that I am in a "classroom lecture on Life & Success". You can't succeed without Failure. Failure is necessary for winning at anything. Failure is necessary for achieving anything. Failure is a door you WILL and MUST go through. Failure is that school of higher learning that you WILL and MUST matriculate through in order to get to where you want to go.

Failure is not for the faint of heart. The pussyfied flee from the mention of Failure's name. The weak Nigga runs, ducks and hides out when even the thought of Failure enters their weak minds. The weak chastise, criticize, ridicule and inwardly laugh at those who are blessed enough to drink from Failure's cup, unbeknownst to them, that they have failed a long time ago in that they chose to play it safe, take no risks, take no chances and live a life with a ceiling, a life of stagnation, a life of mediocrity, a life of under-performance and all their days wishing and wanting in their very core to be successful and have the freedoms, joy and happiness of successful people but are to pussyfied to try.

The winners and successful people are beat up. They have mental and spiritual lacerations, contusions, fractures, whelps, scars and scabs from repeated attempts at "trying". They are mentally tougher and their very demeanor exhibits this. The way they walk. The way they talk. Their vibration. Their energy. Their speak. You can see it oozing from their countenance. They are fearless in the sense that they are "trying" to get where they want to be and are putting forth effort every moment to get there. They seem crazy, abnormal, different and weird because they choose to stand alone rather than follow the masses into the hell of mediocrity.

My first $1.2 Million didn't count

My first $1.2 Million didn't count 'cause I cheated to get it. That was made manifest in the way things went in my life. Anything that starts wrong will end wrong. Anything that starts right will be and end up right. What I throw out into the Universe will come back to me with mathematical exactness. This is Universal Law and can't be bribed or skirted around and everything and everyone in the Universe is under it's jurisdiction.

This lesson was better than any classroom lesson I every attended. My bunkie Crawford told me"

"If it don't hurt..... you ain't learnt nuthin'"

Yes, pain is a motivator and will push you to change, do something different and correct your current course of action, if you are wise. On this go round I am doing things "Right". I am doing this for several reasons:

1. I want to prove to me, myself, Sean X. Gunby, Sr., that I can do it again, the right way, within the bounds of the law, make another Million Dollars;

2. As a result of my past experience, all of the impurities in my mind and spirit have been burned out and no longer exist. I am fully corrected. Fuck being wrong and doing shit the shady, wrong way. This is hard on the mental and spiritual composition of a person. Nothing is harder than doing wrong. It is so easy and internally peaceful to be right and to do right.

3. I want to show America that I can succeed and win within this system as a Black American Male that has despised me since it's inception. That all the road blocks, systemic barriers, STIGMAS placed on me, ostracization, pernicious attempts to destroy me....didn't work. That in spite of and in the face of all of this...... A Nigga can still attain wealth and financial freedom in this muthaphucka. In fact, for a Nigga to do it is even more impressive as The Nigga has to overcome and surmount more obstacles than white males or any other ethnic community, which don't have to confront the same challenges.

Thursday, January 19, 2017

Time is of the essence. My Nigga Black told me "don't let up on your set up". And I ain't for nobody and for no reason. I'm all in. I will get my revenge. I am in the right.

In 2 days I will have completed my entire Federal Bureau of Prisons experience. 5 years 9 months from search warrant, pre-trial investigation, incarceration to supervised release. I walked every muthaphuckin' day down 1 at a time. I bitched, I cried, I hurt, I died, I healed, I laughed, I redefined, I rebuilt, I renovated, I was reborn and today I live! 11x stronger than I've ever been. My best days are in front of me! I worked, I put the footwork in and I am enjoying the fruits of my labor.

Be True!   Be Bold!   Be Aggressive!

Saturday, January 21, 2017

This is my last official day on Federal Supervised Release. My entire Federal case is "ova wit"! From search warrant to pre-trial investigation, to incarceration to supervised release – 5 years 9 months. It's over! One of the greatest learning experiences of my life.

People wish and hope for things they want but are too fuckin' lazy or lack the discipline to get them. Weak muthaphuckas! Get the fuck up off your lazy pussy ass and fuckin' do somethin' to help yourself! Stop fuckin' cryin', whinin', complainin', gossipin', talkin', wishin', hopin', sleepin', and get the fuck up and make it happen.

Tuesday, January 24, 2017

If a muthaphucka bet against me or bet on me quitting, giving up, slowing down, becoming lethargic, inactive, getting high, getting drunk, wasting time, being scared, fearing failure, fearing another human being, losing hope, losing faith, breaking down, getting weak or acting like a bitch or pussy ass nigga – they would be better off and have more fun by riding down the highway tossing their money out the window – at least they could be listening to music while they fuck their money off!

I'm too fuckin' "Right"!!!

Be True!
Be Bold!
Be Aggressive!

"If you do not program yourself....someone else will. You will be programmed. Who will be your programmer?"
-Brutha Victor

On Abraham Lincoln

Speech Delivered on September 18, 1858 in Charleston, Illinois

"While I was at the hotel to-day, an elderly gentleman called upon me to know whether I was really in favor of producing a perfect equality between negroes and white people. While I had not proposed to myself on this occasion to say much on that subject, yet as the question was asked me I thought I would occupy perhaps five minutes in saying something in regard to it. I will say then that I am not, nor ever have been, in favor of bringing about in any way the social and political equality of the black and white races – that I am not nor ever have been in favor of making VOTERS or jurors of negroes, NOR OF QUALIFYING THEM HOLD OFFICE, nor to intermarry with white people; and I will say in addition to this that there is a physical difference between white and black races which I believe will forever forbid the two races living together on terms of social and political equality. And inasmuch as they cannot so live, while they do remain together there must be a position of superior and inferior, and I as much as any other man am in favor of having the superior position assigned to the white race."

Sources:
1. http://www.nytimes.com/1860/12/28/news/mr-lincoln-and-negro-equality.html?pagewanted=all
2. The Strange Career of Jim Crow, page 21 – Woodward C. Vann – "Abraham Lincoln Statement 1858"

At this time, Abraham Lincoln was in a campaign election race for U.S. Senate running against a fellow by the name of Judge Stephen Douglas who was pressing him to take a public stand as to where he stood on slavery and black people. They were stumping throughout the State of Illinois.

"Judge Douglas has said to you that he has not been able to get from me an answer to the question whether I am in favor of negro citizenship. So far as I know the Judge never asked me the question before. He shall have no occasion to ever ask it again, for I tell him very frankly that I AM NOT IN FAVOR OF NEGRO CITIZENSHIP. This furnishes me an occasion for saying a few words upon the subject.

I mentioned in a certain speech of mine which has been printed, that the Supreme Court had decided that a negro could not possibly be made a citizen, and without saying what was my ground of complaint in regard to that, or whether I had any ground of complaint, Judge Douglas has from that thing manufactured nearly everything that he ever says about my disposition to produce an equality between negroes and the white people. If any one will read my speech, he will find I mentioned that as one of the points decided in the course of the Supreme Court opinions, but I did not state what objection I had to it.

But Judge Douglas tells the people what my objection was when I did not tell them myself. Now my opinion is that the different States have the power to make a negro a citizen under the Constitution of the United States if they choose. The Dred Scott decision decides that they have not that power. If the State of Illinois had that power, I SHOULD NOT BE OPPOSED TO THE EXERCISE OF IT. That is all I have to say about it."

Speech Delivered on August 21, 1858 in Ottawa, Illinois

"Now, gentlemen, I don't want to read at any great length, but this is the true complexion of all I have ever said in regard to the institution of slavery and the black race. This is the whole of it; and anything that argues me into this idea of perfect social and political equality with the negro, is but a specious and fantastic arrangement of words, by which a man can prove a horse-chestnut to be a chestnut horse. I will say here, while upon this subject, that I have no purpose, directly or indirectly, to interfere with the institution of Slavery in the States where it exists. I believe I have no lawful right to do so, and I have no inclination to do so. I have no purpose to introduce political or social equality between white and black races. There is a physical difference between the two, which, in my judgment, will probably forever forbid their living together upon the fooling of perfect equality, and inasmuch as it becomes a necessity that there must be a difference, I, as well as Judge Douglas, am in favor of the race to which I belong having the superior position. I have never said anything to the contrary."

Source:
1. http://www.nytimes.com/1860/12/28/news/mr-lincoln- and-negro-equality.html?pagewanted=all

Letter to Horace Greely

Executive Mansion,
Washington, August 22, 1862.

Hon. Horace Greeley:
Dear Sir.

I have just read yours of the 19th. addressed to myself through the New-York Tribune. If there be in it any statements, or assumptions of fact, which I may know to be erroneous, I do not, now and here, controvert them. If there be in it any inferences which I may believe to be falsely drawn, I do not now and here, argue against them. If there be perceptible in it an impatient and dictatorial tone, I waive it in deference to an old friend, whose heart I have always supposed to be right.

As to the policy I "seem to be pursuing" as you say, I have not meant to leave any one in doubt.

I would save the Union. I would save it the shortest way under the Constitution. The sooner the national authority can be restored; the nearer the Union will be "the Union as it was." If there be those who would not save the Union, unless they could at the same time *save* slavery, I do not agree with them. If there be those who would not save the Union unless they could at the same time *destroy* slavery, I do not agree with them. My paramount object in this struggle *is* to save the Union, and is *not* either to save or to destroy slavery. If I could save the Union without freeing *any* slave I would do it, and if I could save it by freeing *all* the slaves I would do it; and if I could save it by freeing some and leaving others alone I would also do that. What I do about slavery, and the colored race, I do because I believe it helps to save the Union; and what I forbear, I forbear because I do *not* believe it would help to save the Union. I shall do *less* whenever I shall believe what I am doing hurts the cause, and I shall do *more* whenever I shall believe doing more will help the cause. I shall try to correct errors when shown to be errors; and I shall adopt new views so fast as they shall appear to be true views.

I have here stated my purpose according to my view of *official* duty; and I intend no modification of my oft-expressed *personal* wish that all men everywhere could be free.

Yours,
A. Lincoln.

Well Abraham Lincoln seems to be a pretty interesting guy in hindsight. He seems conflicted psychologically while suffering much internal turmoil. Who is he? What is his real position? Is he a proponent of Slavery? Or is he a true abolitionist? Can he be called a "people pleaser", saying things to be accepted? An "approval seeker"? Is he a man incapable of making up his own mind and taking a position and standing on it? Is he really a leader with all of his indecisiveness?

I have no problem or qualms with Abraham Lincoln and his beliefs, thoughts and opinions towards me and Black people, nor his thinking and feeling that he is superior to me and Black people. I have no problem with this. That is his opinion. He is entitled to his opinion. His opinion of me is not my reality. In fact, respect has to be given to Abraham Lincoln and any man in the world for that matter who has the courage to say "exactly how the fuck he feels". You have to respect a man like that. Donald Trump, David Duke or any Grand Wizard of the KKK has to be respected for their courage to be honest. It is my belief, that I can get more deals done and more accomplished in a negotiation with this type of person because I know "exactly where he stands" and I will let him know "exactly where I stand" so that we will be able to trust each other.

I would convey directly to Abraham Lincoln, Donald Trump, David Duke or any Grand Wizard of the KKK or any man for that matter, that they are clearly outmatched going up against me in every facet of the word and look each of them squarely in the eye and tell them that "I am better than you and that how you feel about me I feel about you." This would be my opinion. I am entitled to my own opinion. I know for a fact that I'm better than all these aforementioned muthaphucka's.

It's the fake muthaphucka who wears a mask, pretends to be true but is not, and who does what is expedient that can't be trusted. Nothing can be accomplished with this type of person and no deals done. He/She presents an image of solidarity in your face and says all the right things, however, this image just shields his/her true feelings and motives behind a veil.

I remember in the 3rd grade us doing a play about Abraham Lincoln or "Honest Abe" as he is sometimes called, showcasing how great a man he was. That he "freed the slaves" through his execution of the Emancipation Proclamation in 1863/1865; and that as a Black American I was indebted to him and I should honor him for his "freeing" my people. There is the Lincoln Memorial in Washington, D.C. honoring the 16th President of the United States.

You see this is why self-reach education is far superior to the formal education we obtain in the American Public School System. When you "self-reach" you are seeking truth and are essentially a "truth seeker" and can get to the bottom of some shit in it's most granular form. When you go to some else's classroom to be formally instructed you do nothing more than get "that persons or that institutions narrative" on a given topic or subject. And when you are 7, 8, 11, 13 years old that is extremely powerful as you are most impressionable at these ages and receptive to what you hear, see and read.

That's why I tell My Sun the truth about everything now while he is 6 years old. Fuck that... Christopher Columbus was lost trying to get to Asia (India) and was lying to both King Ferdinand and Queen Isabella of Spain and the King of Portugal while taking money from both and promising them treasures, I'm Santa Claus, ain't no Easter Bunny, Christmas is nothing more than the Winter Solstice anthropomorphized. Fuck that! We have to guard our kids minds from bullshit and lies told so that they know the truth from us, the parents. Especially, Black children.

In my opinion!

THE REST OF THIS PAGE INTENTIONALLY LEFT BLANK

MY SPECIAL NAME

Sean K. Gunby Jr

How was your name chosen?

I was named after
my father.

Why is this name perfect for you?

Because it's a good name
and I Love my Dad.

q.brantley

WELCOME TO BACK TO SCHOOL NiGHT!

Dear dad
Thank you for coming
and I love you.

©2012 First Grade Schoolhouse

This the kind of shit you get when you a Bad Muthaphucka like me! Real Shit! This shit REAL!

I Am A Professional Black Father Of A Black Sun!
I Am A Professional Black Father Of A Black Sun!
I Am A Professional Black Father Of A Black Sun!
I Am A Professional Black Father Of A Black Sun!
I Am A Professional Black Father Of A Black Sun!
I Am A Professional Black Father Of A Black Sun!
I Am A Professional Black Father Of A Black Sun!
I Am A Professional Black Father Of A Black Sun!
I Am A Professional Black Father Of A Black Sun!
I Am A Professional Black Father Of A Black Sun!
I Am A Professional Black Father Of A Black Sun!
I Am A Professional Black Father Of A Black Sun!
I Am A Professional Black Father Of A Black Sun!

And I don't believe there is another father on this Planet that is better than me at being a Father. I'mma fuckin' pro at this shit. I'm dedicated to this shit. I concentrate on this shit. Can't nobody fuck wit me at this shit! Show me a Nigga who is a better Black Father than me. Show me any father anywhere in the muthaphuckin' world better than me. You can't find one 'cause it ain't one. I'm the best at this shit. I love this shit.

I was in the Nubian Desert in Kerma, Sudan listening to "Stevie Wonder – As" when I prayed for The Sun, Moon and Stars to give me a Sun. Came back and within that year the Nigga was here! I paid for all of his pre-natal care, vitamins, baby shower, crib, clothes, food, diapers, bottles, everything by my muthaphuckin' self. I changed diapers, gave baths, heated up bottles, woke up 1, 2, 3, 4, 5 in the morning to feed that Nigga, wiped his shitty ass, changed him, put him back to sleep, taught him how to walk, taught him how to play baseball, basketball, football, soccer, wrestling, chess, make him breakfast, lunch, dinner, take him to school, pick him up from school, buy his draws, socks, pants, sneakers, hats, coats, t shirts, computer, bed, bed sheets, taught how to find countries on a world map, addition, subtraction, multiplication, how to find words in a dictionary, Christmas, defend himself, whoop his ass, to think positive, speak positive, self-confidence, believe in himself, dress himself, do his homework with him, how to do pull ups, push-ups and dips, sit ups............ By myself!

Man all this shit. This ain't no game and I ain't playin'. This shit real!

I Am A Professional Black Father Of A Black Sun!

$$$$$$$$$$$$$$$$$$$$$$$$$$$$$$$$$$$$$$$

"The body is the servant of the mind."

As A Man Thinketh, James Allen

WANTED ALIVE

$$$REWARD OF A BETTER LIFE$$$
FUGITIVE

THE BLACK AMERICAN FEMALE (A)

Wanted For:

She is wanted in all 50 states for alienating and isolating The Black American Father from his Black American Male Sun. Filing for child support and other bullshit charges in the white man's court system causing irreparable harm to the Black Father/Black Sun relationship and herself. Hence, she attempts to raise a boy to become a man, not understanding that this is an impossibility for her, that she is not equipped for the job.

The result is a pussyfied, feminized Black American Male child with no energy, no mental toughness, no mental fight, a weakling who hates his mother, hates his father and ultimately hates himself. He is utterly useless because his "mommy" does everything for him even into his 20's, 30's and 40's. He is all the way FUCKED UP! Not long after this comes drug addiction, gangs, no school, no self-respect, no respect for anyone, gun violence, criminal justice system, jail and prison. We have seen homosexuality flourish with Black American Boys without the presence of the Black Male Father.

She is unarmed but extremely dangerous. Her attitude is negative, bitter, shitty and all the way fucked up. She has a real fly disrespectful mouth toward the Black American Father. She blames everyone but herself. She can be found in nail shops, beauty salons and clubs trying to be something that she is not. Fake hair, fake nails, make up and addiction to television, cell phones, Facebook, text messaging is her modis operandi. She hates everything because she hates herself. She loves money and niggas with flashy cars, clothes and jewelry. She is in constant search for the easy way out. She shuns self-reach education, formal education and improving her condition on her own. She can't see that to harm the Black Father is to destroy the Black Male Sun (dummy).

IF FOUND CONTACT THE SUN, MOON AND STARS!

Thursday, January 26, 2017

This life requires dedication, commitment, confidence, vision, belief, faith, footwork, rest, exercise, peace of mind, honesty, etc. I have all these muthaphuckas! I apply them every day. You have to go for what you want! Nobody ain't giving you shit! If anything, they don't want you to move up but stay fucked up, lost, broken, confused, fearful, weak and soft like them! Give niggas like that the stiff arm!

Later on that same morning...........

Everything is going according to plan. Slow and steady. One step at a time. One day at a time. One goal at a time. Be patient, deliberate and execute. Research, examine and study every detail. Leave no stone unturned. See where I want to go in my mind and go there!

Friday, January 27, 2017

I'm up Nigga! Gittin' ready to go hit these windows! I dun built this muthaphucka up to $700 - $800 per week. I'm fuckin' Awesome! I'm on top of this shit! You have to believe! You have to believe 6,000%.

Monday, January 30, 2017

I will do what it takes to win. I will be more prepared than everyone. I will be more disciplined. I will be more aggressive. I will plan tighter. I will be more thorough. I will execute with more precision. I will be in better condition. I will be rested. I will be alert. I will be exacting. I will be prompt. I will be prepared. I will perform. I will be true to me. I am focused. I am determined to win. I will win. I will go pro in the game of life.

On Fannie Lou Hamer

I just so happened to be looking up a scientific equation dealing with mental vibration and pineal gland frequency in **The Universe Dictionary of The Sun, Moon and Stars** and came across a woman by the name of Fannie Lou Hamer..........

This is what I found attached to her bio.......

Courage	=	Fannie Lou Hamer
Bravery	=	Fannie Lou Hamer
Morale	=	Fannie Lou Hamer
Strength	=	Fannie Lou Hamer
Spirit	=	Fannie Lou Hamer
Zest	=	Fannie Lou Hamer
Enthusiasm	=	Fannie Lou Hamer
American Blackness		Fannie Lou Hamer
Energy	=	Fannie Lou Hamer
Fortitude	=	Fannie Lou Hamer
Perseverance	=	Fannie Lou Hamer
Leadership	=	Fannie Lou Hamer
Organization	=	Fannie Lou Hamer
Vision	=	Fannie Lou Hamer
Womanhood	=	Fannie Lou Hamer
Map	=	Fannie Lou Hamer
Agenda	=	Fannie Lou Hamer
Program	=	Fannie Lou Hamer
Itinerary	=	Fannie Lou Hamer
Compass	=	Fannie Lou Hamer
Water	=	Fannie Lou Hamer
Oxygen	=	Fannie Lou Hamer
Determination	=	Fannie Lou Hamer
Focus	=	Fannie Lou Hamer
Impregnable	=	Fannie Lou Hamer
Attractive	=	Fannie Lou Hamer
Gorgeous	=	Fannie Lou Hamer
Patience	=	Fannie Lou Hamer
Discipline	=	Fannie Lou Hamer
Royalty	=	Fannie Lou Hamer
Majestic	=	Fannie Lou Hamer
Black Pride	=	Fannie Lou Hamer
Black Power	=	Fannie Lou Hamer

Damn! I wish I could've met this woman....

December 20, 2017,

To: Ms. Fannie Lou Hamer   **MEMO**

From: Sean Xavier Gunby, Sr.

RE: Black Power

Ms. Hamer thank you for loving me without ever knowing me or knowing that I would even exist. Thank you for your courage, bravery and tenacity. Your oratory skills are par excellence.

I marvel at your inner fortitude and spirit to take a your stand alone. You seemed to have been moved by the "Great Moral Force" in the Universe that is above human comprehension. In 2018, I now listen to your eloquent voice and your command of the Black American vernacular and your supreme ability to enunciate and pronounce that "Down Souf Black American Language" and I'm immediately gripped by the sound of your voice, your attention to detail and my spirit commands me to stand at attention.

Thank you Ms. Hamer ... I am forever indebted to you. My Sun, Sean Xavier Gunby, Jr. is indebted to you and the children that are in his children's scrotum are indebted to you.

I wish I could've met you. To ask you "How did you muster the courage to say what you said? How did you harness the mental toughness to endure the physical torture you unjustly received? **How? How? How?** I ask myself.

But you know what? I think I already know. It's that Black American Nigga Strength that no other ethnic group possesses or understands (not even the African in Africa), it's uniquely ours, that says "I can't let these muthaphuckin' crakkas beat me... Fuck these crakkkas!"...... Yeah I understand fully well. I've been there!

Ms. Hamer, I love you and I honor you.

Sean X. Gunby, Sr.

Tuesday, February 2, 2017

All the while I was looking to and for something "external" to me to inspire me, to define me, to give me fortitude, strength, confidence, belief. Whether it was another person, Black History, cars, clothes, money, sexual relationships, God or whatever. NONE OF THAT WORKED. It took me to lose everything I had of material value or "value less", my freedom and access to My Sun to realize, understand, overstand and know that it's "ME" I have to look to for inspiration, definition, fortitude, strength, power, confidence and belief. It's "internal"! It's "ME".

Sunday, February 5, 2017

If you want your situation changed?? – You have to change that muthaphucka yo-self! Fuck waiting on somebody, someday, some year, some month, some time, some circumstance – FUCK THAT! Change that muthaphucka immediately! It's up to me! I will decide and can't nan-nutha-muthaphucka stop it! I got it!

"If you do not program yourself...

someone else will.

You will be programmed.

Who will be your programmer?"

-Brutha Victor

Sunday, February 12, 2017

In the midst of a custody battle for My Sun. I make no more deals, I fear no more, I hesitate not again, I'm cautious no more – I will not be bullied with My Sun by his mother never again. A paradigm shift is in motion and taking place. I will not run. I will stand and fight. Within the bounds of the law I will fight to the death. Yes, I am willing to die for custody of My Sun. My namesake. That's My Sun!! Given to me for FREE by The Sun, The Moon and The Stars. I am responsible for him. The Universe has entrusted me with his care. I will not let The Universe down. I am a Dad! To My Sun I am "Daddy". That's what he calls me. I am a Black Father of a Black Sun! I am Somebody. I am his Father and I will be respected as his Father. I am Somebody!

Monday, February 13, 2017

When you are a "Black American Male convicted felon" in this world – you must believe in yourself 6x more than ever. This confidence and belief must be total and wholly exclusive. The population at large, your family, "friends" and casual acquaintances will judge you and expect you to continually and perpetually be held hostage to your felony conviction, feel shame, guilt and remorse for your own self. That you should "remain in your place" and never assert yourself or demand total respect as you have lost that inherent and innate right to love yourself because The United States of America has labeled you as a convicted felon.

What is happening here is that the majority of the population at large has a bullet in their heads called "I hate myself and my life so let me find somebody worse off than me (perception only) and stomp them to make myself feel better." This is a mental narcotic. This is a spiritual opioid. And the majority of society is addicted, hooked, strung out and high as a muthaphucka off this drug.

Actually though, from my experience, the former inmate is a better quality of human being and better positioned to live successfully.

He/She knows loss, self-examination, scolding oneself, reflection, truth in self, killing oneself (spiritually & mentally), re-gestation of oneself, giving birth to oneself anew, rebuilding oneself, renovating oneself, and ultimately redefining oneself. He/She knows self-discipline, calming the mind, calming the spirit, resting the body, resting the mind, patience, physical fitness at the highest level, spirituality, integrity (your words and actions being everything and meaning something).

The majority of the society doesn't – which is why they are outmatched when they go up against the convicted felon. Fuck what America and society thinks. I will define who I am!

Wednesday, February 15, 2017

In this muthaphuckin' (world) you can't ever relinquish, voluntarily surrender or give away you backing of your own self! You cannot. You must always have your back. You cannot go against yourself. If you do, then you will consistently, repeatedly and most times get fucked around by society and the people in it. And the "Tremendous Moral Force of The Universe" will not come to your aide as it does not help weakness.

Conversely, if you have your own back and fight back, resist and stand on your square – muthaphuckas will ponder thrice before engaging you – your getting fucked around will be kept to a fraction and the "Tremendous Moral Force of The Universe" will come and assist you and augment your spirit and soul and make you fuckin' invincible.

Thursday, February 16, 2017

Where are you? Who are you? What are you about? Where are you going? What is your plan? What are you working on?

The overwhelming majority of people you meet and encounter on a daily basis are utterly and completely "aimless". The are on somebody else's time. They are programmed by someone else. They are incapable of planning. They lack discipline. They are easily distracted and sidetracked. They show that they are more interested in cell phone apps, social media, TV, sex, and reality TV personalities than they are in their own children, grand-children and their own lives. This is across all racial, ethnic and socio-economic backgrounds. They are completely fuckin' lost. They are walking dead people. They are just waiting to die. They have no hope. They have no faith. They have no vision. Their spirit is mangled and broken.

They have allowed some circumstance or "life experience" to destroy them. It knocked them on their ass and they lay there and won't get up crying like a little bitch! From the outside they look good but it's a mask. They drive expensive cars, wear name brand clothes and shop in expensive stores. They are "dressed up garbage cans." They present to the world that they are aplomb, bold, brave, courageous, imbued with fortitude, determination, spirit, perseverance and strength. However, as you will observe over time – (as time reveals all) – they are really shaky, insecure, indecisive and weak muthaphuckas. Fakers!

Stay away from these lower level creatures and gravitate toward exceptional superior beings like me.

We (Black America) Don't Have To Hate White People To Get To Where We Want To Go

We don't have to hate white people to get to where we need to be. We don't have to remain in constant lamentation about the slave trade, what white folks did to us? Slavery?

Fuck that shit! That shit is ova wit! It's the past! It's gone! Never to come back. Unless we allow it. We have to learn from that shit. Fuck white people and what they are doing. Fuck the Chinese and what they are doing? Fuck the Russians and what they are doing? Fuck North Korea and what they are doing? Fuck the whole world and what they are doing.

We have to focus on ourselves and what the fuck we are doing. We have to focus on our own game irrespective of what the world thinks. Us sitting around in the barbershop, beauty salons, barbeques, family reunions and Thanksgiving/Christmas dinner talking about "white folks and what they did 300 years ago, 3 years ago, 3 hours ago or 3 minutes ago ain't about shit"...

Fuck them. They are focusing on their game as they should. China is focusing on their game as they should. North Korea is focusing on their game as they should. Russia is focusing on their game as they should.

When achieving a goal or playing any sport, game or competing for anything, when you begin to focus on your opponent(s) game, and not "your game" ..you fucked up, you've lost. In chess, you have to watch what your opponent does and make moves to thwart his every attempt to check mate your king, BUT YOU HAVE TO WATCH WHAT THE FUCK YOU ARE DOING AND MOVE YOUR PIECES TOO... YOU HAVE TO FOCUS ON YOUR GAME!

Our heads are so fucked up about some "past shit" that we can't move forward. It's like a 31-year-old still crying or complaining about their high school sweetheart and when they broke up after 4th period by the cafeteria. That Nigga is FUCKED UP!!! STUCK LIKE CHUCK! That's precisely where we are as a "collective". Still crying about some slavery shit of yesteryear like some bitches... We can't get nowhere like that. Shut the fuck up.....get up off the mat.....sniff your smelling salts.....drink you some water...and keep fuckin' moving forward... FOCUSING ON YOUR OWN GAME!!!

We don't have to fuckin' stay here if we don't want to. NOTHING IS HOLDING US BACK FROM LEAVING. Evidently, from past experience, maybe America ain't the best place for us as a "collective". We have theoretical, empirical and practical experience here that shows conclusively that this ain't the spot. Perhaps we can do better in another region of the world as a "collective". What about going back home to Africa and starting all over from scratch. Build our own nation and call it "BLACK AMERICA", "NIGGA WORLD", "ANEW LAND", "BLACKNESS" or whatever we decide.

Come up with our own central bank, our own currency, our own stock exchange, commodities exchange, grow tomatoes, corn, beans, peas, wheat, apples, grapes, oranges and sell them to the world. Make our own automobiles, washing machines, stereos, cell phones, toilet paper, tampons, bra's, draws, soap, tooth paste and sell them to the world. DO SOMETHING FOR OURSELVES instead of begging the white man to take care of us.
TAKE CARE OF OURSELVES instead of relying on the white man to take care of us. FEED OURSELVES instead of begging the white man to feed us.

We (Black America) some stupid muthaphuckas (myself included because I still live here too). We force ourselves on the white man and demand that he accept us. This ain't our country. I don't give a fuck how long we been here and what blood we've spilt here, what we built here and what contribution we made here. North America is the home of and belongs to the Native American/Mexican and all the ancestors/relatives before the European ever came here. Yeah I know some of you Niggaz gonna say *"Yeah. But the Black Man/African was here back then too…"*. Yeah I've done that research too. And my 5% Bruthas will talk about the Asiatic Black Man and how we were everywhere on the planet all up in Europe etc…. I agree, and you are correct that the African/Black Man did have contacts with the Native Americans Before Common Era (BC), but at the end of the day … We, the Black American, are from Africa. That's where other Africans captured us and sold us into slavery.

The white man don't have to accept us here. Let me say that shit again. The white man DOES NOT have to accept us here. This is his shit. This is his apartment. This is his house. We were brought here by force under his employ to work. We were brought here as "the help". So how the fuck can we ever expect that the white man is going to somehow cede and bequeath his project to us? Won't happen.

Example:

You have your own crib (apartment, house, condo) and you pay all the bills in that bitch. You put the security deposit down, mortgage down payment, pay the rent, pay the mortgage note, you furnished that bitch, did renovations, hung the drapes, put down the carpet, pay the water bill, EVERYTHING IN THAT MUTHAPHUCKA you do. One day, a cousin, relative or friend calls and says "Yo.. I need a place to stay for a minute until I can get my shit together.."… You say "Cool".. They move in and stay longer than they said, don't pay no bills, eat all the food and now want you to move out of your shit so that they can stay there. They force themselves on you and in your personal life. They want to borrow your car or pick them up here, take them there. Don't contribute shit to the household and beg you take care of them.

That's precisely what the fuck Black American's are doing here in American as a "collective". Stand the fuck up Nigga!

Clarification:
When I speak of "white people" I speak in general terms as describing the "ruling party" here in America as a "collective". It is not lost on me that there has always been, going back to the 15th Century during the slave trade, white people who empathized with the Black American, did not partake in his subjugation or slavery and spoke out against it as morally wrong.

Just as today in 2018, there are many, many, thousands, hundreds of thousands and millions of white people here in America that think, feel and know that they way Black Americans are treated, especially The Black American Male, is all the way fucked up and don't like it. There are white people here that would rather live in peace with the Black American Race rather than constant tension with this "race shit" constantly on TV, Internet, etc.

But as a Black American Male, it's hard to discern which white people are good and which are not.

THE BLACK MAN HAS GOT TO HELP HIMSELF AND STOP BEGGING THE WHITE MAN.

I propose these images/faces on our own currency.

BLACK AMERICA'S INTERNATIONAL CURRENCY CALLED:

"THE ADVANCEMENT"

$1 Bill	"Richard Pryor"
$7 Bill	"Dr. King"
$13 Bill	"Malcolm X"
$20 Bill	"Fred Hampton"
$50 Bill	"Huey P. Newton"
$100 Bill	"Muhammad Ali"

Have our own shit! Quit begging another muthaphucka for shit we should be doing ourselves. Weak ass muthaphuckas.

Stop fuckin' crying and get to work and leave white folks alone.
Stop forcing yourself on them. They don't have to accept you.
Nor should you need any muthaphucka to accept you. Git Right
Nigga and accept yourself and build your own shit.

═══

I got summoned by telekinesis just a few minutes ago to appear
before The Sun, Moon & Stars.

Sun, Moon & Stars: Sean Xavier Gunby, Sr. we summoned you
here to make a proposition to you;

Me: Thank you for allowing me to live in your
Universe and I try everyday to live up to
your expectations of me. I am at the
ready to hear your proposition;

Sun, Moon & Stars: We offer you the opportunity to re-do your
life and come back and start over as a
child as someone else, a different ethnicity,
a different socio-economic background,
change your life any way that your heart
desires, different color or anything you
wish;

Me: In all due respect Sun, Moon & Stars, I
thank you for your offer, but I must decline
changing anything about me or anything
that has happened to me. If you are so
inclined as to let me re-do my life I request
that you make me a Black American Nigga
all over again. I wouldn't want to change
not 1 thing. I love all Niggas, and above
that I love being a Nigga!

We (Black American Niggas) are the strongest of all the ethnicities that exist on Earth. Our perpetual struggle against adversity is the germination of our strength. It's the same as when you take a piece of black dirty coal and put it under extreme pressure......it transforms into a precious diamond. Also, when you train a muscle in your body.....it needs resistance to grow...the more resistance the bigger the muscle.

We are physically superior to all ethnicities that exist on Earth including our cousins in Africa. It was something about the "triangular slave trade route" and the slave trade that made us spiritually, mentally and physically tougher than everyone else. We are more beautiful, more muscular, talented, gifted and age better than any other race of people on Earth.

So, with all due respect Sun, Moon & Stars, I must decline your proposition to change anything. I am happy and I love being a Nigga!

Sun, Moon & Stars: You are doing an excellent job! Peace out!

Me: Black Power!

Friday, December 22, 2017

Man listen... No matter fuckin' what you better believe in yourself! I don't give a fuck what just happened, what's finna happen, what happened last week, what happened 4 hours ago, what's going to happen later this evening, what's going to happen this weekend, what's going to happen next month.... You gotta fuckin' believe in yourself! It's tantamount to any type of peace of mind, contentment, progress, success, goal achieving and happiness. If you got this, you are on your way..... NUTHIN' can stop you. NUTHIN'!!!

Without a healthy sense of confidence in yourself, void of any belief in your own abilities, if faith in yourself is absent.... YOU FUCKED UP!! You ain't goin' nowhere. You ain't accomplishin' shit. You ain't finna achieve a muthaphuckin' thing!

You know what's finna happen to you?

You are getting ready to be programmed by someone else. You will be a spoke in somebody else's wheel, a tool in someone else's tool box. You will be paying mental rent to someone else scared to death to take any type of calculated risks. You never will be able to compete wit a Nigga like me who ain't got nuthin' but supreme confidence in his abilities. You aint' got a muthaphuckin' chance.

You better "git right" or get used!

Sean X. Gunby, Sr.

I've read this book in it's entirety at least 3x in my lifetime and the muthaphucka is always Bangin'! I wrote these down on April 11, 2015 while I was in The Feds. The book of which is speak is:

The Autobiography of Malcom X As Told To Alex Haley
Copyright 1964 Alex Haley and Malcolm X
Copyright 1965 Alex Haley and Betty Shabazz

"But it is only after the deepest darkness that the greatest joy can come; it is only after slavery and prison that the sweetest appreciation of freedom can come."   **Page 387**

"We will meanwhile be working among our own kind, in our own Black communities – showing and teaching Black men in ways that only other Black men can – that the Black Man has got to help himself."   **Page 384**

"I told the Englishman that my alma mater was books, a good library. Every time I catch a plane, I have with me a good book that I want to read – and that's a lot of books these days. If I weren't out here every day battling the white man, I could spend the rest of my life reading, just satisfying my curiosity – because you can hardly mention anything I'm not curious about. I don't think anybody ever got more out of going to prison than I did. In fact, prison enabled me to study far more intensively than I would have if my life had gone differently and I had attended some college. I imagine that one of the biggest troubles with colleges is there are too many distractions, too much panty-raiding, fraternities, and boola-boola and all of that. Where else but in prison could I have attacked my ignorance by being able to study intensely sometimes as much as 15 hours a day."   **Page 183**

*"In the hectic pace of the world today, there is no time for meditation, or for deep thought. A prisoner has time that he can put to good use. I'd put prison second to college as the best place for a man to go if he needs to do some thinking. If he's **"motivated"**, in prison he can change his life."*   **Page 398**

"Children have a lesson adults should learn, to not be ashamed of failing, but to get up and try again. Most adults are so afraid, so cautious, so "safe", and therefore so shrinking and rigid and afraid that it is why so many humans fail. Most middle-aged adults have resigned themselves to failure."   **Page 418**

"But Malcolm said to hell with that! Get up off your knees and fight your own battles. That's the way to win back your self-respect."   - By Ossie Davis   **Page 464**

Where yo abs at Nigga? Shiiiiiitt if you ain't got no abs you ain't got that muthaphuckin' look! THAT MUTHAPHUCKIN FED LOOK!! Big chest with big arms wit a pot belly gut ain't about shit...You just a boiled egg with legs…….

Saturday, February 18, 2017

If you are living your life based on what another muthaphucka says, thinks, feels or implies or suggests, then you are a lost creature parked in neutral. Get the fuck outta my way 'cause a Nigga like me is coming through focused like a muthaphucka. Time is ticking – keep fuckin' wastin' time and you will soon be in the company of woulda, coulda, shoulda, regret and remorse.

Sunday, February 19, 2017

It is beyond my comprehension how I am going to be required to pay child support?? I am the primary care giver for Sean. I have my own 2BR apartment for him and I. I don't need, want, have or receive any public assistance. I stand on my square and "get down for my crown." His mother (My Sun) is a total bum. That's what the fuck it is. I call it like I see it. She can't take care of herself or her kids. I took care of her. I was good to her. But that meant absolutely nothing to her. She turned on me and betrayed me and our son like nothing. Cooperated with the Feds to help send me to Federal Prison and "took" or "stole" custody of My Sun (in the white man's court system) 27 days before I was to self-surrender to prison.

She can never "take" or "steal" custody of My Sun in the eyes of The Universe, The Sun, Moon and Stars. Never. While I was in prison, My Sun's love for me never dissipated, it was only enflamed higher and made more robust in spite of a deliberate attempt to capture his mind and turn him against himself and turn him against me.

Let me digress a minute……………

On June 12, 2015, I got my 1st and only visit during my entire incarceration in prison. It was a Friday. At FCI Morgantown we had visitation on Friday, Saturday and Sunday only. If the warden decided to cancel visitation for whatever reason there was no visitation. It didn't matter how far your family travelled to get there, how much they spent, what they sacrificed… no visitation.

I had been telling my mother for months that I wanted to see Lil Sean and if she could please bring him to see me. She said she would if I could arrange the logistics of the trip. She lives in Georgia and Lil Sean at the time was living in Clifton, New Jersey.

A "pivot moment".... The Sun, Moon and Stars revealing itself to me by human means...

One of My Main Muthaphuckin' Niggas, a Nigga by the name of Patrick C, who lived in the Bronx, whom I had befriended several years prior even before I caught my case was who I reached out to. He had already put about $100 on my books as soon as I got to prison and had sent me in some Options Trading Books from Amazon.com as well. I called Patrick and asked if he could bring my Mother and My Sun to Morgantown, West Virginia to see me and that we would pay him whatever his expenses were, gas, hotel accommodations, his food, and his valuable time. Just name the price. Patrick said he would.

My mother (72 years old at the time) arranged to fly up from Atlanta, GA to Newark, NJ, whereby she would meet and pick up Sean, Jr., meet up with Patrick and they would drive the 6.5 hours to see me.

Wow... this shit brings tears to my eyes as I'm writing this shit now. Today is Monday, December 25, 2017, Christmas Day, and Sean, Jr. woke up with his "Daddy" in our apartment today and opened up his Christmas gifts that his Black Santa Claus brought him. I watched him open up every muthaphuckin' toy as if it was the last thing I was going to do on this Planet.

I spoke to my mother via telephone on Thursday, June 11, 2015, the day before my visit, and she told me that she had arrived in New Jersey and was at the hotel, that she had spoken to My Nigga Patrick and that everything was set for them to pull out the next morning headed to FCI Morgantown so that I could see My Sun, who I hadn't seen in 8 months since the night I dropped him off and boarded a 1-way First Class flight to Charleston, West Virginia to self-surrender and begin my 18 month sentence.

I was fuckin' floating on Cloud 32! My Mother and My Sun were both coming to see me in less than 24 hours. DAMN!! I do have a life outside of this prison.

One thing that was real for me while I was incarcerated was that you become so programmed and institutionalized while you are in there, caught up in the "prison politics", that sometimes I lost touch with the fact that "I actually have a life outside of this muthaphucka" and just the thought of seeing My Sun and My Mother made that manifest and tangible for me.

Well never a dull moment with me.

I had had this weightlifting "weight pit" rivalry going on with another inmate for the preceding 8 months and we were always "talking shit" to each other about who could hit the most weight, who looked the best and just testosterone masculine Nigga shit. Well, that Thursday, about 1 – 2 hours after I had got off the phone with my mother confirming their arrival the next day and my visit, this dude tried to hit some weight on the bench press and missed it. I dug into his ass talking mad shit about how he missed that certain weight and I had hit that shit months ago. We had done this to each other before even when I tried to hit some weight and missed it. I kept going, I kept going, I kept going fuckin' wit 'em.

I was on my way to Main Line for lunch and saw him again talking to 2 of his tight partners. I walked passed them and said something again. This struck a nerve with him and he hollered out "YOU FAGGOT!". When I heard him say this it was like someone had shot a rod of fire through my mind. I was stunned. I was shocked. My ego was fuckin' hurt. His 2 partners heard it. One was 22 years in on a 30-year bit, a real "OG" and his other partner was 8 years in on a dime.

As soon as the sound of the last consonant came out if his mouth I had turned around and started walking back toward him knowing that I couldn't let that ride, no way no how. Nah.. Niggas had heard this shit. What they gonna think of me? They were gonna think I'm soft. As I was walking back toward him about 6 – 7 paces – YOUR VISIT TOMORROW – YOU SEE SEAN XAVIER GUNBY, JR. TOMORROW. YOU SEE YOUR MOTHER TOMORROW. YOU HAVEN'T SEEN SEAN JR IN 8 MONTHS. HE'S BEEN LOOKING FOR YOU. YOU GET TO SEE, HOLD AND SMELL YOUR SUN TOMORROW. This shit came right to the front of both sides of my left and right brain. I paused then turned around and went to Main Line to eat lunch.

My head was fucked up while I was eating. My ego was fuckin' wit a Nigga something fierce. My pride was bruised. I was in prison and let a nigga talk to me like this. What the fuck? God Damn!!! Ahhh man...

I ate my lunch, dumped my tray exited Main Line headed back to the Unit where we both lived scared, confused and mad as a muthaphucka. As I got to the hand ball court about to turn up to go to the Unit, the dude that called me a faggot had met me there, walked up to me and said *"Yo I apologize man…. I shouldn't have said that"…* *"Yo I apologize"..*

Now my head is even more fucked up now.. Damn.. this Nigga dun' came and apologized to me? Why? Is this some game? I thought this was supposed to end with a fight or us having forever tension forever. Am I a pussy for not swinging on him? Is he a pussy for apologizing? Wow! This is some different shit. This is new.

Well I was to later find out that this happened a lot in prison and I had one more situation that required same. I've seen 2 dudes get into a heated "verbal altercation" that didn't turn physical …….."yet"… Then you see one of the partners/homies of one dude or the other act as a mediator to chill shit out and approach both dudes to see if the tension can be deaded. I've then seen the 2 dudes go into the card room or study room alone, close the door and stay in there for a while talking and clearing the air, come out, the static is gone, and nobody lost respect.

The few fights I seen or heard about at FCI Morgantown most times leads to somebody snitching to the CO about who was fighting, both dudes get packed up and sent to the SHU "the hole" (23-hour lock down), stay in the SHU for months with minimal phone and mail contact and then they ship you to another prison somewhere else in the United States, you lose good time credit and can possibly catch another charge (assault) lengthening your sentence.

Anyway…..

I avoided the catastrophe of missing my 1 and only visit and learned some valuable lessons in the process.

1. Be careful about what you say to people, how you talk to people and "playing with" people because things can go from being playful to super serious quick;
2. There is nothing weak or feminine about going to another man or anyone for that matter that you have an issue with and talking it out before it gets ugly – communication is everything;

3. You never know the mind state of the next man/woman, what bad news he/she just got, what they are going through, so it's best to lead out with respect because the slightest bit a disrespect can get you into an ugly situation;

Friday came and they called my name over the loud speaker "Sean Gunby report to visitation". I had already left the Unit and was waiting down by the chapel so I wouldn't have to walk that far to see My Sun and my mother.

I will never forget this as long as I live. I walked into the visiting room, saw my mother and my little cousins she brought with her and I saw Lil Sean. I said "What's up Man!!!" like I always had said for the 1st 3.5 years of his life and he just looked at me. He didn't run to me and jump in my arms which was his favorite thing to do. He didn't say "DAAADDDDY" which was his favorite thing to do. He just sat in his seat and stared at me not knowing what to think or do. This fucked me up! Shook me to my core. I immediately went over to him and picked him up and said "What's up man".. He looked me in my eyes, smelled my breathe and smelled me and instinctively knew that he was being held by his father. He warmed up to me after that. We went and got some chips and candy out of the vending machine together and just walked around the visiting room. I saw my mother, she had aged but was looking good and healthy for 72.

The visit lasted about 1 – 1.5 hours and my mother said that Patrick was on his way back to get them. My heart shattered. They were leaving. Ahhhh man. I kept it together as they walked out the door. I was cool 'cause I knew they were coming back tomorrow, that Saturday. I walked back to the visiting room entrance, they patted me down and searched me and I walked back across the compound to the Unit. I was emotionally fucked up. I went back to my cube, took my clothes off and slept for like 2 – 3 hours. I used to wonder why dudes would come back from a visit and immediately go to sleep. I understood then. The visit in prison was emotionally taxing and draining as a result of all the emotions one feels during the visit (elation, excitement, happiness, joy, humanness again, exhilaration and sadness post visit and then realizing your immediate reality). That shit is a muthaphucka.

Saturday came, I was up at 5:07am which was my everyday get up time, did my reading and writing, worked out and got dressed and ready for my visit. "Sean Gunby report to visitation". They patted me down and searched, I walked into the visiting room and Sean Jr. flew into my arms "Daddy". That's what the fuck I'm talkin' bout!!! I said to myself. We visited for a while, maybe 45 minutes and my mother said "Well we finna go 'cause Patrick gotta drive us back to New Jersey..." It was like someone had stabbed me in my soul with a pair of scissors. I was heart-broken. They were leaving me for good this time. I was staying, and My Sun was leaving. Tears started to well up in my eyes. I told my mother "I have to go to the bathroom ....I'll be right back."

I wasn't coming back. I couldn't make it back. I couldn't watch them leave. I didn't go back. I ducked around the corner by the CO to get patted down, wiped my eyes, took a deep breath and said "C'mon Sean you gotta walk back across this muthaphuckin' compound into the Unit so Nigga you betta Git Right!!!." And I did. I never went back to say good bye to my mother or My Sun. I went back to the Unit and slept for about 3 hours. This was a "pivot moment" during my incarceration because it reminded me that "I had a life waiting for me in Jersey."...

I began to study harder, read more, work out harder, become more disciplined, more patient and more "RIGHT" than I already was. I was going to make it back to Jersey to get My Sun.

I began to meditate and visualize that I'mma still make it. I won't let this hinder or stop my game. I won't let up on my set up. I've come too far and been through too much. If I quit, give up and be nothing than my haters win. That won't happen. I won't let it happen. When I succeed, as I'm doing now, they lose. They will lose betting against me. I ain't nuthin' to fuck wit. All I do is rise!

I have control over my thoughts, my vibration and my energy. I am master of myself. I prepared for this in prison. I'm ready for whatever. Strength, courage, fight, dig, fortitude, attitude, determination, will, faith in myself will get me to where I want to go. I have opportunity all around me. Everywhere there is golden opportunities. I met a lot of Bruthas in the joint who are doing or have done 2, 4, 7, 9, 12, 15, 18, 22, 25 years and would willingly change places with me no questions asked. I am in a great place. My best days are in front of me.

My Muthaphuckin' Nigga Patrick C picked up My Sun and my mother in Newark, NJ, drove them to 6.5 hours to Morgantown, West Virginia on Friday, stayed the night, took them the next day to see me, picked them up and drove them back to Newark, NJ that Saturday evening and didn't ask my mother for a dime. He did that shit on the strength! Word is Born!! Nigga did that shit from the heart for a Nigga. That's a muthaphuckin' true friend. The definition of A Real Nigga!

Monday, February 20, 2017

Ain't no way possible that I'm just gonna lay down and let a bitch handle me and bully me with My Sun! Ain't gonna happen. Whatever the fuck I gotta do to maintain control of My Sun's life I will do even it that's giving my life. I am his father and I'm somebody. I am somebody! Any nigga that let a woman "run him" when it comes to his kids is a pussy ass nigga in my opinion. You never have seen and never will see the lioness in running the pride. It's the male lion that dominates.

Tuesday, February 21, 2017

Man this shit don't stop! The hustle is ever present.

Wednesday, February 22, 2017

It's time to make this shit happen! This phase of where I am in my life is preparatory, transient and ultimately temporary. I have a plan that I am executing. The plan demands patience, perseverance, determination, discipline, spiritual, mental and physical stamina and endurance. Even though I know this phase of window cleaning (which I have grown from nothing to something) is temporary; I will still go hard as a muthaphucka at it 6,000% effort from wake up to 9 o'clock count.

Things take time. You have to be able to wait. Patience, waiting and time are greater than Hannibal and his entire army. Waiting is an art. An art that I developed and mastered in federal prison. The mind has to be regulated, controlled and told to shut the fuck up! Proper rest and sleep, reading and physical exercise aide and augment your ability to wait.
Furthermore, I must have a vision and a plan on how to get there. This is not easy. You have to have a lot of balls to want to win.

Friday, February 24, 2017

I have a plan and that feels good. It's comforting to know. On low days when I'm not feeling it, I always remind myself – "You got a plan Nigga" – "You are working on somethin'" – "You are not just out here aimless". I am my #1 fan. My greatest cheerleader. I believe in me and what I'm doing, and thats all the fuck I need to hit my target. I will achieve **all** of my goals before I am old.

Talked to my Bunkie last night and he told me "use your head for something more than just a hat rack." – Yeah!..... I needed that.

A Nigga got to love himself/herself and stop expecting love from anyone outside of his self/herself. They will never be able to give you the love you need and is required. The more you look for it "outside" of yourself – the more you will stay "fucked up" and lacking. Give yourself that shit and fuck what anybody thinks. They don't give a fuck about you anyway. Most likely they don't want you to raise your vibration and leave them behind. They would much rather prefer you continue to "go against yourself" & "abandon yourself" and stay down in the basement with them fucked up with no map and no direction. You will never catch Sean G partaking in some shit like that! I'mma Black Super Hero Action Figure!

Sunday, February 26, 2017

Yeah! Nothing can stop me from doing what I want to do and accomplishing what I want to accomplish. My best days are in front of me! You have to always believe in yourself. It's so important. Guard you mind from weakness and the thoughts of lesser weak people.

I can't wait and I am so looking so forward to self-publishing this book and selling it. I can't fuckin' wait to hold my first copy in my hand.

If you can keep your head when all about you
Are losing theirs and blaming it on you,
If you can trust yourself when all men doubt you,
But make allowance for their doubting too;

If you can wait and not be tired by waiting,
Or being lied about, don't deal in lies,
Or being hated, don't give way to hating,
And yet don't look too good, nor talk too wise:

If you can dream - and not make dreams your master;
If you can think - and not make thoughts your aim;
If you can meet with Triumph and Disaster
And treat those two impostors just the same;

If you can bear to hear the truth you've spoken
Twisted by knaves to make a trap for fools,
Or watch the things you gave your life to broken,
And stoop and build 'em up with wornout tools:

If you can make one heap of all your winnings
And risk it on one turn of pitch-and-toss,
And lose, and start again at your beginnings
And never breathe a word about your loss;

If you can force your heart and nerve and sinew
To serve your turn long after they are gone,
And so hold on when there is nothing in you
Except the Will which says to them: 'Hold on!'

If you can talk with crowds and keep your virtue,
Or walk with kings - nor lose the common touch,
If neither foes nor loving friends can hurt you,
If all men count with you, but none too much;

If you can fill the unforgiving minute
With sixty seconds' worth of distance run -
Yours is the Earth and everything that's in it,
And - which is more - you'll be a Man my son!

"If" – is a poem by British Nobel Laureate Rudyard Kipling, written in
1895. The poem, first published in Rewards and Fairies (1910), is written in
the form of paternal advice to the poet's son John.

On The Black Church In Black America

As far back as I can remember going to church on Sunday's with my mother in the 1970's and 1980's, whether that was in New Jersey or when I went "down sowf" to South Carolina or Georgia, "the Black Church" was the place where you saw everybody you knew, cousins, friends, yo kin folks (as the old people would say), relatives, neighbors, acquaintances and strangers.

I hated going to church because the kids in my neighborhood would be playing tackle football (kill the man with the ball), stick ball or riding their bikes at the precise time that I was leaving or in church. I remember I used to fake like I was sick every Sunday morning. I was fine, healthy and strong all week all the way up to Saturday night. Sunday morning, I was sick, and I would fake throwing up or I would get the thermometer out of the medicine cabinet and turn on the stove and slide the thermometer back and forth over the heat until the temperature got up to 101 or 102 and then I would go show my mother that I was sick and that she should understand that it wasn't in my best interest for me to go to church that Sunday. She **ALWAYS** saw right through that bullshit and needless to say I was in the backseat of that 1976 Chevy Impala on the way to church.

The Black Church, to me, in my experience, was simultaneously a boring and an exciting place. The shit was boring when they went down the itinerary of remarks, welcomes, taking up collection, and even the preacher when he did his sermon screaming, yelling, spitting, sweating, wiping his forehead with his handkerchief, saying "amen", "y'all don't hear me dis moaning", "can I git a witness", "Jeeeeeeeeeezus"... Him asking for an amen from the congregation and parts of the congregation giving him "amen" feedback. This shit was confusing to me but entertaining.

The exciting shit was when the choir sang and if they had a Nigga on the piano or organ who could play that muthaphucka "Right", the piano/organ Nigga *"could capture the entire congregation up in a rapture"* and consequently, have them in the palm of his hand and could make all dem "holy roller sanctified" Niggas do what he wanted them to do for as long as he wanted them to do it. All dat Nigga had to do was keep playing and leanin" on them piano/organ keys. Now when the piano/organ Nigga was doin' his thang, inevitably, some older Black woman/women who was/were well known in the church would catch the "Holy Ghost" and start boppin', jumpin', swingin', shoutin', hollerin' for Jeeeeeeeeeezus!!, and go into an uncontrollable convulsion almost seizure like dance. This was confusing to me, nevertheless, I found it fascinating.

She/They would jump on you, knock you over, step on your foot, slap you with the Martin Luther King, Jr or John F. Kennedy fan and be out of control as long as dat Nigga on the piano/organ kept leanin' on that muthaphucka. I liked this part. Actually, I loved to see somebody catch the Holy Ghost and then imitate them later at home. That shit was some exciting shit to see. Then some of the ushers would have to come "fan" the Holy Ghost catcher after the piano/organ Nigga slowed down. It was funny to see the logistics work when it be 4 – 5 Niggas be dun caught the Holy Ghost but only 3 ushers. Somebody wasn't gonna get fanned and cooled down and if dat piano/organ Nigga crunk dat shit back up (the piano/organ Nigga would make you think he/she was finished and finna stop playin'…..then all of sudden dat Nigga a-lean back into that goddam piano/organ and throw them Holy Ghost Niggas back into another frenzy for Round 2) and it would be back on in that muthaphucka. I loved watching this. Loved it.

To really see this shit on a professional level, you have to go down into the deep south in one of them old wooden churches "back in da bushes". Up North Black Churches are like high school level action cause they try to be all sophisticated and shit, but when you get "DOWN SOWF" in the deep south, that's that Professional Black Church shit.

I always liked to eat at church especially down sowf, 'cause you ain't had no Soul Food until you dun had some muthaphuckin Soul Food from down sowf. That's where the shit started at. And everybody brings a dish for the whole congregation to eat after church. Muthaphuckin' collard greens and shit, REAL BAKED macaroni and cheese, black-eyed peas, that good muthaphuckin' down sowf country ham with the pineapple on dat muhhhphucka, rice and gravy, soft-ass cornbread, string beans, cabbage, sweet potatoes and you may even find some muthaphuckin' hog maws and chitlin's in that muthaphucka!! Red velvet cake, chocolate cake, REAL MUTHAPHUCKIN" DOWN SOWF BANANA PUDDING (Niggas up North can't make no muthaphuckin' banana pudding, you gotta go down sowf for dat shit), lemon cake…. Ahhh man.

Yo.. My Mother makes the best muthaphuckin' hog maws and chitlins in the world Nigga. I like that way them muthaphuckas smell and stink up the whole house. Put some hot sauce on them muthaphuckas…… GOD DAMN MAN!!! Some good eatin' Nigga.

But this is the shit that always puzzled me about the Black American Church????

No matter if I was in a Black church up North or Down Sowf, we always prayed to and saw images of a "white Jesus". On the stained-glass windows, pictures on the wall, images in the bible, everybody was white but all I saw was Niggas in church. This shit perplexed me. I ain't white so why am I praying to a white Jesus? Ain't no pictures of no white people in my house, so why am I praying to a white Jesus? Why doesn't my God look like me? Why ain't my God a Nigga wit a afro or fade like me? Why don't my god have BIG pretty lips like me? Why my God ain't brown like me? I always questioned this and wondered .."Damn, that's why Niggas fucked up cause even God don't like us"

However, after doing some "self-reach research and study" (which I suggest you do), I began to understand the process. When we were sold into slavery by our own-selves, or captured by the white man, or whatever fuckin' story you believe, when we were brought here as a "conquered people", over time and generations we lost all concept of who the fuck we were. The slave master doing what was in his best interest gave us these images of white Jesus' and white angels and white characters in the bible were played by white Hollywood actors on TV.

This shit is worse than shooting cocaine, heroin, battery acid and unleaded gasoline into your cerebral cortex.

Damn we fucked up! And we ain't got nobody else to blame but ourselves.

Tuesday, February 28, 2017

It has been those most painful experiences of my life that have taught me the greatest lessons and perfected my spirit, built my character and made me the strong Nigga that I am. In the midst of these challenging times you could never have made me see or understand that I was growing and that I would emerge stronger as a new creature, spirit and mass of energy vibrating on a higher frequency ready to ascend and elevate higher than I was before.

Case in point, at 48 years old, I feel, look and think better and clearer than I did at any point in my life. I have more energy, mental toughness, endurance and stamina than at any point in my life. That's in it's entirety (mentally, spiritually and physically) I feel unlimited – bound by nothing but my thoughts and my belief in myself. What I want to do I can do! What I want to have I can get! What I will to happen will happen! What I strive for will be gotten! Whatever the fuck it is that I want to materialize – all I have to do is "set that shit in my mind"! ... and ... It's done!

Friday, March 3, 2017

To My Niggas In The Feds!

Get prepared for your release. Prepare now!! Plan now. Decide now! Think now! Be ready when you go to R&D! As far as "this society" is concerned – in my opinion – there is very little if any – redemption opportunity given to the convicted felon. Very little understanding or empathy. It will be incumbent upon you and you alone to redeem yourself, to understand yourself, to give yourself a 2nd chance, to accept yourself and ultimately define yourself.

These (most) civilians are going to judge you, look at you with a tone of condescension, be skeptical of you, fear you, and distance themselves from you. You will have done nothing but be true, bold and real (as you must in The Feds). Truth of the matter is – is that they are weaker than us. They are false, untrue and untrustworthy. They will tell you that they will call you back to your face and won't. They will look you in your face and tell you that they are going to do something for you and won't. They do not value the words that come out of their mouths. Integrity is in absentia. They lack the courage to say what the fuck it really is. Remember!! It's not you – it's them.

I have found that the most "realest" relationships I have had and still have is the ones I made in prison. In prison, at least I maintained, your word "meant somethin'" or "it better" mean somethin'. What you said better be that. It's not like out here in society. These muthaphucka's weak.

Get ready for that. Be prepared.

Monday, March 6, 2017

Sometimes life has dealt me a blow or a punch in the mouth that took me from being my #1 supporter to my #1 hater! I used to stay stuck in this train of thought for extended periods, spiral down and crash & burn. Not no more though! Fuck that shit! That pattern of thought is useless and detrimental to my existence. Today! I examine, probe and thoroughly inspect what the fuck it is that has me thinking and feeling down, look at it, acknowledge it, honestly accept it and then discard that shit and keep pushing forward!

Sunday, March 12, 2017

I am a Professional Father. Moreover, I am a Professional Black American Father of a Black American little boy of 5 years old. Period! Ain't no question about it and I don't need any type of sanction, degree or approval from anyone to be that. I am that!

Furthermore, I love being a Professional Black American Father. It's an amazing opportunity and experience. Nobody……Nobody will ever stop, prevent or hinder me from being same – not even his mother! Period!

"DISCIPLINE"

Webster's New World – College Dictionary 4th Edition

Discipline – 1. A branch of knowledge or learning. 2. Training that develops self-control, character, or orderliness and efficiency. 2b. strict control to enforce obedience 3. The result of such training or control; specifically self-control or orderly conduct.

Sean X. Gunby, Sr.'s definition

Discipline – 1. Doing what the fuck I got to do within the bounds of Universal Laws. Minding my muthaphuckin' business. Staying out the way and out of other people's business. 5 – 7 days of exercise per week.

7 – 8 hours of sleep every night at the same muthaphuckin' time. Steel trap mind set. Accepting nothing less than respect. Taking my time in all areas of my life. Waiting. Being patient. Not allowing myself to be distracted.

Tuesday, March 6, 2017

One step at a time. My new success is assured. Just because I don't see tangible results every day, doesn't mean I am not progressing. As long as I am not moving backwards in reverse. I'm back on my hustle. Back on my Fed Shit. Staying focused and disciplined. Seeing the "long haul" vision not instant gratification. Knowing that my vision will materialize over time and that is ok. I have time. No rush. Take your time Sean.

Wednesday, March 15, 2017

It doesn't stop! Ever! The concentration. The dedication. The discipline. The consistency. The perseverance. The self-control. Being efficient in all my actions. Being a man. I control how I see me. I am in control of my self-perception.

I do not have a Facebook account. I do not have an Instagram account. I am not on social media at all. It is a total and complete distraction and waste of time. I can't afford it.

This is a fun part of my comeback journey. I control my destiny. They will marvel and discuss my comeback for years into time.

Friday, March 17, 2017

Today I was ordered to pay child support of $68 per week. The court ordered this. My Sun's mother sued me for same. I won though. She lost. As she knows I took care of her and all her kids. She has to go to sleep and wake up knowing that and knowing that the Sun, Moon and Stars know this as well and that she will have to "true it up" with them. The Sun, Moon and Stars sees everything.

I have never ducked My Sun. I have been the majority financial provider for My Sun since before he was born. Me! Nobody else! Me! It's ok though I feel liberated now that I got this shit behind me. Now I will re-focus back on "My Master Plan" and put myself in a position to get custody.

I'm built to last. My best days are yet to come!

Thursday, April 27, 2017

I see defeated people every day. I encounter them. I can tell from their posture, demeanor and speak, that they are mentally and spiritually injured. Some may be "passing thru" a stage or experiencing a "life moment", whereby life has punched them square in the mouth and they are flat on their backs dazed.

Some will eventually rise and will never be the same. Some will be worse off and never recover. Some will lay flat on their backs for the remainder of their natural lives and never do anything.

A certain few, an extremely small percentage, will rise up, levitate, shake it off, GET RIGHT and be masters. I fall into this category.

Nobody gets out of this thing called life without getting wounded spiritually and mentally. Nobody!! But you must get the fuck back up and keep pushing!

Sunday, April 30, 2017

Hung out with My Sun all day. Laundry, rode his bike, played catch, played baseball, soccer, wall ball, he/we read 2 books, spelled some words, ate clean and just did boy stuff, man stuff – Nigga Shit! I see my impact on his life & character. I am making a difference and it don't take much money at all. Just time. He doesn't pay attention or listen all the time – but I understand he is only 5 – 6 years old. I'm on him and I'm on him tough! This ain't no play-play Sesame Street shit. This is real world Black Male Nigga shit. I love it. I am a full time Professional Father period!

A Letter to Trayvon Martin

Today is your birthday and you are 23 years old. You still exist to me. I fell in love with you. I didn't know you, never met you, never saw you in person, yet, I fell deeply in love with you.

They hurt me Trayvon. The State of Florida and the United States Department of Justice. They fuckin' stood by and watched and made 2 wrongs out of 1 wrong.

You was mindin' your own business. You were where you were supposed to be. Just tryin' to git back to your Father on your way back from the store. Just being a 17-year-old kid, full of life, possibilities, freedoms, opportunities, potential, dreams, imagination, vigor, life, zest, enthusiasm, energy, vibration and love.

I couldn't believe the verdict man... "NOT GUILTY" and he went free the very same day and was given his gun back that he assassinated you with. I couldn't fuckin' believe it Trayvon. I was hurt to my core. Baffled. Despondent. Dazed. Angry. Rage. The United States of America did it again via The State of Florida. They displayed to the Planet Earth that a Black American Male's life is of no value to them, the United States of America. They told me again. They have been telling me my whole life. Just look at American history. It's all there.

But anyway.....forget them and back to you.

I love you man. I will never ever, ever, ever, ever, forget you. I know you would've been a strong Black Man.

I miss you and I love you Trayvon.

Sean X. Gunby, Sr.

Tracy Martin and Sabrina Fulton I mean no disrespect.

A Letter to George Zimmerman

You preyed on a adolescent child who had just been 16 and was only 17 by 3 weeks. Maybe 140lbs. Just a child. You hunted him down. You snuck up behind him from the back. Trayvon was unarmed. You were armed.

You weak. You a chump-ass muthaphucka. Hoe-ass, bitch-ass faggot.

Hey bitch-boy.

Let's me and you re-enact that same night you murdered Trayvon but this time it will be me and you. I will be unarmed and you can be armed. You can sneak up behind me and grab me and let's go for what we know and may the best man win. **I'mma Stand My Ground"**, and I'mma take that gun from you and put in your mouth and blow your muthaphuckin' brains out.

Sean X. Gunby, Sr.

I'm moving. I'm moving forward. The progress "appears" slow – extremely slow – but I know 1 thing for sure --- I am moving forward! I have a plan. I have an agenda. I have an itinerary. It's time to let go of worthless emotions related to "past people".

I like my life where I am and what I'm about. Slowly, but definitely surely.

Peace

I Must Control The Deepest Perception of Myself

I have come to know, over time, that it is incumbent, mandatory and imperative that I, Sean X. Gunby, Sr., control the deepest perception of myself. That I must protect, guard and shield my mind from "attempted impressions" made by people, situations, occurrences, life experiences, circumstances, stereotypes or whatever. I must exercise the mental discipline, mental toughness and mental strength to thwart attempted impressions from outside of me.

It is I that should tell me who I am. It is I that should tell me what I am. It is I that should tell me how great I am. It is I who should tell me my limitations. It is I who should tell me my abilities. It is I who should tell me my potential. It is I who should tell me my capabilities.

What someone else expects, what someone else says, what someone else does, what someone else implies, what someone else forecasts for me, what someone else pontificates about me, what someone else conjectures about me, has no bearing on my reality and doesn't mean a muthaphuckin' thing to me.

What you think about me is none of my business.

I am about the business of being a "Professional Life Liver". Every muthaphuckin' day I wake up, I make a decision to live that day as a Pro. I'm remain vigilant that "my perception of me is what counts most", "my perception of me is what's most important" "my perception of me trumps everyone else on the planet".

I can be and I am somewhat open to "constructive criticism" provided I feel it's sincere and coming from someone who has real world experience in whatever they are pulling my coat too. I listen, run it up the flag pole, examine it, analyze it, examine the source, analyze the source and "receive or discard" based on my examination and analysis. I repeatedly see and hear people speaking to, giving suggestions, disseminating advice and flat out telling other people to do something a particular way or go about something this or that way and they themselves DON'T HAVE NO TYPE OF MUTHAPHUCKIN' experience, know how or surface knowledge of what the fuck they are giving advice, information or suggestions about.

I am the fool if I entertain these people.

I will control the deepest perception of Sean X. Gunby Sr.

Monday, February 19, 2018

I continue to maintain my focus and discipline keeping my vision in tact and clear. I kill weak thoughts before they take shape; I do not allow them a chance to breathe or take part in any of my "self-conversations". Strong, positive thoughts are given free will and the latitude to move about at will. They are encouraged and nurtured to fruition and the physical manifestation of the vision in my pineal gland.

Pineal Gland – Often referred to as "The Seat Of The Soul", "The 3rd Eye" or "The 1st Eye". The size of a grain of rice that sits in the center of the right & left cerebral cortexes. Produces a natural hallucinogenic known as dimethyltryptamine or DMT. The Ancient Nubians/Egyptians had elevated its use to where they were able to harness it's powers do supernatural things, astral travel and transcend this world.

Everything is moving forward according to my map, plan and itinerary. I am actually ahead of schedule. Which is good. I continue to eat clean, get my proper sleep, exercise daily and mind my muthaphuckin' business. I am having the best time of my life watching Lil Sean grow and blossom into a 7-year old. He is strong, alert, spritely, nimble, aggressive, loquacious, precocious, inquisitive, engaging and eager. Right where he should be.

Time is of the essence! Time is of the essence. There is no time for fuckery, buffoonery, stagnation or complacency. Now is the time for industry, single-mindedness, building, constructing and fulfilling the life that I want to live; cause make no muthaphuckin' mistake about it; I AM GOING TO GET THERE!

You Have to Speak It Up

This is a Universal Law and cannot be bribed, bought or circumvented. This is as real as The Sun.

Whatever it is that you desire to transpire or take place; you have to speak that shit up! You have to speak it into existence. You have to continuously, repetitively and consistently speak and talk about what you are in the process of doing and where you are going. Furthermore, you have to speak that shit in the tone and inflection that it is a foregone conclusion and it is guaranteed that this vision or that event is going to take place.

Let me clarify some shit before a muuhhfucka get what I'm saying fucked up, confused and twisted and fails to get the results. I do not mean speaking up an idle wish, dream or fantasy sittin' on yo ass with no effort or footwork behind it.

You have to speak it up and then "get the fuck up off yo ass" and make that shit happen. Move toward your speak up. Work toward your speak up. Push toward your speak up. Discipline toward your speak up. Be diligent toward your speak up. Envision your speak up. Be patient toward your speak up. Plan toward your speak up. Map out your speak up. Exercise toward your speak up. Get physically fit toward your speak up. Eat clean toward your speak up. Git rid of fake muthaphuckas blocking your speak up *regardless who the fuck they are*. They must go! They can't stay! Surround yourself with other "speak up muthaphuckas" you know so you muthaphuckas can constantly speak it up to each other. If you can't find no other speak it up muthaphuckas around – then just keep speaking that shit up to yourself!

If you follow and adhere to the aforementioned maxims I just outlined. 10 out of 10 times you will acquire whatever it is you speak up.

One muthaphuckin' thing for sure tho is -------

You never stop speaking it up!

Monday, February 26, 2018

Tremendously successful day. I ate clean (bowl of oatmeal, 3-5 cups of coffee, hummus, chicken breast, beans, water, collard greens, sweet potatoes). Worked out. Cleaned windows, picked up Lil Sean from school, helped him with his homework, cooked us dinner, wrote on my book, got 1 new YouTube subscriber, uploaded a YouTube video and thought strong muthaphuckin' thoughts all day. A total success.

The game is still on. Execute the plan Sean. Stay out the way Sean. Time is of the essence Sean. Crush the competition Sean. Stay focused Sean. Remain disciplined Sean. Be patient Sean (one inch at a time).

I'mma bad muthaphucka!

Tuesday, February 27, 2018

I put on another stupendous performance today in my life. I am a professional at living life. I AM a Professional Life Liver! Let me expound on same:

I woke up and read something positive and motivational which I do every morning after I make me a cup of coffee. Did 640 reps of ab work. Got Lil Sean up, got his clothes out, put him in the shower and made him some grits, eggs and bacon (crushed up for him all in one pile...he likes it like that), got dressed and dropped him off to school. Did my window cleaning route (made $205). Picked Lil Sean up from school and we came home.

I'mma muthaphuckin' pro at this shit! I'm disciplined! I'm focused and I'm destined to find a glorious end and etch my name into the mental fabric and souls of Lil Sean's grandchildren.

Working on this book that you are now reading (Volume Muthaphuckin' II). This muthaphucka is going to be a bad muthaphucka too. I am a writer. Moreover, I am a fantastic writer. I'm getting a lot of love and positive feedback from these "Millennial Muthaphuckas" (ages 17 – 29) on my Volume I book. I repeatedly hear from them that they love my straight up honesty and realness and my will to succeed and not give up. They also like my choice to not "just get a job" but to start something and work at it.

See these young muthaphuckas don't want no bullshit and they haven't been conditioned to fear anything yet. They are reckless chance takers and know no fear. Reminds me of me back in 1987 – 1996, back when I was the age of what would have been considered a Millennial. I think we were called GENERATION X. Yeah that's it.. We didn't give a fuck either about saying or doing whatever the fuck. That's a fun age to be. You don't care. You just don't care except for what is immediately in front of you and you are willing to try anything and you are looking for answers, clues and solutions.

As you get older, in your 30's – 40's, there is a tendency to become "conservative", less of a risk taker and more pussyfied fearing you may lose "something", whatever the fuck that something is? You begin to see the pessimism in everything and what can go wrong and become afraid to try anything. You fall in line with the masses, you conform to societal norms, and become depressed, obese, full of anxiety, worry and fear taking a whole bunch of medication. In other words, YOU BE FUCKED UP!

I rebel against allowing myself to conform, full of fear and worry, to become pussyfied and afraid to take risks (legal...not illegal) and try different shit, different ways, different paths. Fuck it! This is what leadership calls for. Leaders try different things everyday in different ways. Leaders buck conventionality. They dance to their own music.

Napoleon Bonaparte:
  "Circumstances-what are circumstances? I make circumstances"

I fucks wit dis type a shit!!!!!! Fuck that shit. Draw that shit up in my mind and then set about the task of making that shit happen and manifest into reality. Speak that shit up!

It's good to be me!

You Are All The Way Fucked Up, Your Life Is In Shambles And Life Has Punched You Square In Your Muthaphuckin' Mouth And You Are Down In The Dirt!

Ahhhhh man. Ha Ha Ha!!! LoLOLOLOlllololoLOL... Damn man, I'm not laughing at you. Calm down. I can laugh about that shit now 'cause I went through the exact same shit a few years back. Lololololololololololol. I think everybody gets a turn because one thing for sure is that NOBODY is getting out of this life without some mental and spiritual contusions, lacerations, fractures, whelps, concussions, rips and punctures. NOBODY! No matter how well people wear their mask, the truth is always there.

The critical point here that I would like to discuss with you is:

1. What do you do?
2. Can you survive it and continue to "live"?

In my opinion and in my experience, this is the most fertile soil to plant new seeds and grow a new you. This is the best time to excavate, rip down and demolish your old you and rebuild, renovate and build a new you. This is the best time to lay a new foundation made of black granite. This is the best time to lay the groundwork for a re-definition of who you are and what you are about. You are the closest to success than you've ever been when you are here. This place has OPPORTUNITY written all over it. It is these moments, these occurrences, these "life experiences" that provide the optimum time and best environment for "change". You see, you are already fucked up and fucked around down in the dipsey dumpster all the way in the muthaphuckin' basement. Nobody is around to help you because everyone who you thought loved you and was your "friend", has abandoned you, left you, dropped salt on you, crossed you, betrayed you, dissed you, shitted on you, is talkin' shit about you, left you for dead and written you off as a loser.

Here is when the lights are the brightest. It's show time. This is a very critical time. It's sudden death, win or lose, sink or sail, live or die, showdown, death or survival for you.

You can give in and quit. Go out like a bitch! Like a weak muthaphucka, cry, lay down, put on the cloak of self-pity, why me? Pick up your blame thrower and blame everyone else for your condition and cry like a little pussy muthaphucka! And you will prove all the betrayers, fake friends and family right. They will be right and that will be your legacy. Your legacy will be:

> **That weak ass nigga went out like a sucka. That bitch quit and gave up.**

And that's where you will stay for the rest of your life unless you decide to "git right".

CONVERSELY

You can be like me, Sean X. Gunby Sr., and you can start from right the fuck where you are, all the way fucked up, and you can begin to put the pieces back together ONE AT A MUTHAPHUCKIN' TIME. You examine and analyze yourself thoroughly to the muthaphuckin' core. You ask yourself the tough difficult questions of:

How did I get here? What happened to me? Why did I do this to myself? Who do I have around me? And then ultimately, How do I get the fuck outta this circumstance?

You do searching, fearless, relentless, root uprooting inventory and cleansing. You vow to yourself that you will make it. You forgive yourself, hug and kiss yourself and tell yourself "It's OK…. We got this… We can do this". You set about the task of self-transformation and self-transmutation. You kill, murder and assassinate the old you to make way for the birth of the new you. You begin to eat healthier, exercise every day, get 7-8 hours of sleep every night, cut off associates and acquaintances that ain't about shit. You affiliate with Real Niggaz; Niggaz who about somethin', that are going somewhere; Niggaz that have direction, aim and purpose. Write down a plan of action, a map, itinerary. Command patience to manifest in your minds eye. Command discipline to show up for work every minute of every day.

Once you have your map, plan and itinerary, you must execute that muthaphucka with acuity and precision looking neither to the left nor right but straightway head to the sky. Guard your mind and control the deepest perception of yourself and fuck what another muthaphucka got's to say about you that they can't say to your face. Fuck 'em! You have your marching orders. Be continually grateful because your circumstance could have been a whole lot worse and more fucked up than it is. Yes! Be Grateful.

Dry your tears and tell the world to "Watch out Muthaphucka I'm comin' through and if you in my way I'mma run right the fuck ova you!!!Move Nigga!!!!"

Peace out

That Muthaphuckin' Fed Nigga
United States Federal Bureau of Prisons
FCI Morgantown, Morgantown, West Virgina
Gerard Unit – B Wing "The Ghetto"
Sean X. Gunby Sr.
Reg#: 65932-050 "Jersey"

Friday, March 02, 2018

7 good solid hours of sleep last night.. Nigga feelin' refreshed, rejuvenated, undefeated and alive. I'm up. I'm up and at 'em. Got a few windows to knock out today, going to the muthaphuckin' gym and show them cologne and perfume wearing muthaphuckas how a real Fed Nigga work out, then I pick Lil Sean up from school and we gonna chill all weekend. I have Lil Sean for the next 5 days straight (I have 15 overnights per month; exactly 50% and I pay no child support. I filed a motion MYSELF to get off that shit).

Anyway, it's good to be me! I have a great life! Everything is going according to plan, I am on track and on schedule. Time is of the essence and this shit don't stop. I have no time for lethargy, complacency, stagnation, apathy, wishing, obesity, laziness and wasting time. I must move and I must move NOW!

I am 48 yrs old, will be 49 in 9 days and I look fuckin' fantastic. I'm doing better than most people who have not had to deal with the setbacks, reverses, discrimination and other obstacles that I've had to overcome.
That's because I'm better than them. I'm stronger than them. I'm more resilient than them. I embrace failure, they succumb to failure. I never give up and am always optimistic, they quit and see the negative in everything. I have a plan, map and itinerary coupled with the discipline and the spiritual, mental and physical stamina and endurance to execute same; they are aimless and directionless, lack discipline and weak, spiritually and mentally broken, obese and fat and have no energy to do anything but to wallow in their self-loathing and self-rejection.

You have to get the fuck up and make shit happen. You have to MOVE! You have to ACT! You have to INQUIRE! You have to be AGGRESSIVE! It is your responsibility to make manifest of your vision. It is your responsibility to make real your dreams! It is your responsibility to create a plan. It is your responsibility to execute your plan. And I don't want to hear that "I'm too old" shit, "I have kids" shit, "I don't have time" shit. Those are muthaphuckin' excuses for your own pussyfied under-performance and under-achievement. You fuckin' lazy. You weak. You have too many minds *(too many different issues, relationships, distractions going at the same time)*, you are addicted to your cell phone, you are fat, you are lazy, you are obese, you have no energy, your thinking is fucked up and negative, you allow fear to rule your life. All of these can be remedied and cured. *"Wherever the sickness is…there lies the cure"*. You have to heal yourself! Nobody cares and nobody is going to do it for you.

Peace out Niggaz!

Friday, March 02, 2018

I feel undefeated! No that's a lie.. I feel unfuckindefeated! Nothing is impossible for The Black God. Nuthin' is unaccomplishable (is this a word?...fuck it if it ain't I made it up)!!! Nothing is too far fetched for me. My imagination has no boundaries and is infinitely expansive! My spirit is robust and augmented by my belief in myself! My confidence in myself is supreme! My future is whatever the fuck I want it to be. All I have to do is imagine it, envision it, think it and then I manifest that shit with ease!!! I'm fuckin amazing!!

Anyway… That's how the fuck I think and feel right this second. And my thought and feeling is TRUE!

On Monogamy

Who invented this fictional, unnatural and unrealistic ideology and then mandated its adherence in real world human relations? It was then purported to be something that can be easily implemented into one's psyche and behavior by the use of one's judgment and reason. It is erroneously held over the male participant in relationships like the Sword of Damocles. It is the "defining desideratum" in which a male's loyalty is judged. It is the supreme unwritten and unspoken expectation of all men by their female counterparts.

Let's examine this more closely….. I will if you will allow me the latitude….. Thank you

My position is that there is no such "real" practice as Monogamy in the Universe. My position is that this is a fictional, made-up practice that is as unnatural and unreal as a unicorn or mermaid. My position is that it is impossible for any male living organism in the Universe to be monogamous, as we were not intended to be such, hence, pro-creation. Somehow monogamy has been conjoined and ingratiated in religion and put on the same plane as a moral law or moral consideration.

There is no fowl in the air, fish in the sea, reptiles, mammal on land or any living organism for that matter that is monogamous. It is always the case whereby the "dominant male" has more than one female companion in his arena. This is his role decreed by The Sun, Moon and Stars.

Here lies the problem……….

With all the aforementioned organisms, fowl, sea creatures, fish, mammals, reptiles; the males of each of these respective groups are "open and notorious" with their roles of having and choosing several females to round out his arena. There is not hiding, sneaking, lying, mask wearing or none of the other weak shit that male humans do in order to live up to a fictional ideology that who the fuck knows from whom or where it came from. The alpha male lion, cape buffalo, ostrich, penguin, duck, goat or whatever, will pridefully, boldly and with strength show that he is capable of maintaining his "manhood rights". And the women in his arena "love him for his masculinity and his manhood". For all women always prefer, desire, crave and love "a Real Man".

This is where male humans fuck up.

These stupid muthaphuckas, weak ass muthaphuckas lie and promise their female friends some shit that they are inherently by nature incapable of doing. They look these women straight in the eye and say "I will only sleep with you". LYING MUTHAPHUCKA! YOU LYIN' MUTHAPHUCKA!

Scientifically and biologically a man cannot control "when his nature will rise". It is futile and impossible for a man to attempt to mentally control his nature from rising. If he sees an attractive woman and she makes "any type of move or gesture" that she is "wit it"; there is nothing he can do.

He can be truly in-love with his wife and happily married, however, if this woman walks up to him and brushes up against him, looks at him with sensual eyes or grabs his dick, there is nothing he can do. It's ova! He will most definitely have a universally natural sexual experience with that woman and he is well within the Laws Of The Universe in doing so.

For me, I cannot ever tell a woman that I won't fuck another woman. How do I know? How can I tell who I will meet? How? In all of my relationships I make that very plain and put it right out on the floor at the very beginning when the topic first arises. I say "I cannot promise you that"......"Now if you need to hear that then you need to go find you a lying ass Nigga who will lie to you and tell you he will......but he won't"...

Women have it in their minds that if a man fucks another woman that he is somehow "dis-loyal". This is a fallacy. This is the furthest thing from the truth. Monogamy CANNOT BE EQUATED with loyalty. They have nothing to do with each other. Loyalty is a whole nuther discussion.

I think I have covered and drilled down into this topic of Monogamy well and am satisfied with my discourse on same.

Thank you for listening

Sean X. Gunby Sr.

In the same vein............

Most men are so pussyfied, weak, effeminate and fake that they do not possess nor can they muster the balls and courage it takes to be 6,000% honest with their woman or women in general. They "wear a mask" and present the image of what the woman wants to see and then once they "sneak & steal" the pussy under the cloak of deception, manipulation and lies, they remove the mask and show that they ain't shit, never was shit and ain't gonna never be shit. Real Niggaz tell a woman straight up what the fuck it is and let their "honesty" be the honey that attracts the bees. Honesty is attractive and respected worldwide.

You tell a bitch straight up that all you want is some pussy and to go out and have a good time every once in a while, you want some thought provoking, insightful, high vibration intelligent conversation and companionship. You want loyalty and honest dealings and that you will reciprocate same........ most mature women will agree to this deal.

Most woman understand that in 2019, everyone is busy and free time is a luxury and commodity that has to be exploited and used to the max. So there is no time for "hide and go seek" with the pussy. She understands because she has a life and is busy as well. And who doesn't want some throw down, sweat dripping, dirty talkin' name callin', hard core fucking? Who doesn't want that? Everybody wants that!

Friday, March 09, 2018

Peace! I'm executing my plan. I'm following the map I drew up to a "T". I'm not allowing anything or anyone to distract me. I allow nothing to interfere with my itinerary. I evade and thwart all attempts to get me off my game. I remain vigilant and understand fully that my life is my responsibility and that it is up to me if it is going to be. I must bring into existence the type of life, lifestyle and legacy that I want to live. I am 8,000% responsible for same.

I don't blame anything or anyone for my shortcomings, failures or setbacks. I look at myself and examine my myself carefully and thoroughly and ask myself "What the fuck happened Sean?" "What did you do Sean?" "What could you have done better Sean?" and then I tell myself "Prepare better next time Sean" and move forward with the lesson and wisdom in my mental bank.

My YouTube Channel "Gunby Publishing" is doing extremely well. I am closing in on 100 subscribers. That will be a milestone for me. I continue to accomplish whatever I put my mind to. Nothing is out of reach for me. Nothing is impossible for me.

Tuesday, March 13, 2018

My birthday was 2 days ago. I turned 49 calendars. I am the best I've ever been. I am in the greatest physical shape of my life, I eat better, I sleep better, I think better, I calculate better and I'm just all around more efficient as a "Professional Life Liver".

The more ripened I get the more amazing I become. My concentration and focus is at an all time high. My ability to get things done seems to get better with each day. I'm more able now to block out distractions and expunge unnecessary people from my life with no 2nd guessing. I am fully aware and more cognizant that time is of the essence and every day must be utilized to the fullest. There can be no time wasted on meaningless interactions and conversations. Everything and everyone I encounter must have potential for spirit elevation and raising our vibrations. We don't fuck wit muthaphuckas who ain't about shit. These spirits are strictly avoided.

The building of my legacy is in full effect and I will engrave my soul, life, name and accomplishments in the mental chambers and hearts of my great grandchildren. For their entire lives here in this Universe, they will always have a vivid, real and true reference point of a Strong Black American Male, their great grandfather, who rose, fell, regrouped, rose again and overcame obstacles which appeared unsurmountable and succeeded against all odds. This way they will know that the blood that is necessary to accomplish such great feats is running through their veins and that they are bound by nothing.

I will instill in Sean Xavier Gunby, Jr. all of the necessary mental toughness, stamina, endurance, heart, will and abilities to achieve whatever it is he so desires. Focus will be on proper diet and rest, scheduled reading, extreme physical fitness programming and spiritual correctness and reverence for The Sun, Moon and Stars and that The Universe is the Supreme Law to be adhered to. Sean Jr. is already 8x better than me and way ahead of where I was at 6 years old. He holds forth amongst his peers and is more advanced experience wise than his classmates.

Raising My Sun is not a game, Sesame Street or a play-play thing.

This shit is Real!

Peace out!

Another day won. Another strong performance from Sean X. Gunby Sr. in the game of life. Woke up after 7.5 solid hours of restful sleep, made Lil Sean some grits, eggs and bacon. Put him in the shower, got his clothes out for school, drove him to school and went and did my window cleaning route. Finished up my route, went to the gym and did 11 sets of (10 push-ups, 10 pull ups and 10 dips with 30 second rest in between) then hit the spin bike for 5 miles and got up outta there.

Sold 2 books and got 3 new subscribers to my YouTube Channel (Gunby Publishing – aSTIGMAtism In My Soul TV). Not only am I selling books everyday on my window cleaning route or wherever I am (grocery store, laundromat, gym, Walmart, Kmart, etc.), I am also now selling/pushing my YouTube Channel to up my subscribers to get the product out there. I am having so so much fun with this book and YouTube Channel that you wouldn't believe. I'm meeting all types of people from all walks of life from all over the planet.

It's amazing that just by starting something new in your life so many avenues and opportunities open up for you. I have no idea where this book is going to take me but I'mma ride this muthaphucka out til the end! The fact that I have no idea what I am doing is what is making this journey so exciting and interesting. I'm just about finished with this book and will be publishing it in about 3 weeks. I will do a lot better with this book (Volume II) than I did with Volume I, in that I now have some experience on how to market, promote and sell my books. I already have an established "reader base" that will buy Volume II on "GP" and being curious as to what I have to say now since they've already read Volume I.

I am full of life, my vibration is high, my frequency is elevated, I'm The Best Muthaphuckin' Window Cleaner on the Planet, I'm a Professional "Life Liver" and most importantly I'm a Professional Black Father. I have a dope life and it's good to be me.

      Be True!
              Be Bold!
                    Be Aggressive!

Peace to the Gods

"It's Weak To Speak And Blame Somebody Else....When You Destroy Yourself"

Axiomatic, profound, a maxim and has proven to be self-evident in the current state and condition of Black America.

Words from the Hip Hop Lieutenant Commander, the living legendary Chuck D, front man for the Rock N Roll Hall of Fame inducted group, Public Enemy. These lyrics are off the track "Welcome To The Terrordome" on the album "Fear of a Black Planet", released in 1990.

I have followed closely, admired, been a fan of and been inspired by Chuck D and Public Enemy since 1986-1987 when they disseminated their first LP "Yo! Bum Rush The Show". These Niggas snatched Hip Hop by the throat in 1987 – 1988 and held in a choke hold for a solid 24-month period. In my opinion, there never was before, has not been since and will never be another Hip Hop phenomenon like Public Enemy. Public Enemy "turned the channel on the Hip Hop TV" and made us all watch another program that was far more relevant, profoundly important, utterly serious and antibiotic to Black America's sickness and illness of lack of knowledge of self, self-love and self-pride.

Forever and repetitively the supreme pro-Black force in Hip Hop, Chuck D and Public Enemy, continually reminded us and highlighted many of the historical systematic transgressions carried out against Black America. He told us of the current traps and future plans for Black America without Black America's input and that it was incumbent upon Black America to do what was necessary to survive.

However and as you can see from the title of this section of my book, Chuck D didn't relieve Black America from it's responsibility of self-preservation. In fact, he makes it super plain that we owe ourselves first, that Black America must take care of Black America first and that nobody is responsible for Black America but Black America.

Additionally, he puts the onus squarely on Black America as says:

> it's weak to speak and blame somebody else...when you destroy yourself........

This is self-explanatory and needs no further illumination. Let's examine Black America now from several perspectives now.

Black Fathers

Black fathers abandoning their post in an act of treason to himself and Black America. Whether it's a case where there is a break-up or separation from the mother of his children, or the Black fathers repeated attempts at illegal criminal activity which requires him when caught to be imprisoned for extended periods away from his children, or he just having committed spiritual and mental suicide and given up. In my opinion, this is at the crux of our self-destruction.

Look at little Black boys ages 7 – 24, in a lot of cases they are fucked up! Their spirit has been broken or never even inserted in them by their father, they are mama's boys, aimless, directionless and hopeless. In a lot of cases, not all (calm the fuck down)! The Black Father in a lot of cases is missing in action. Him and him alone can remedy this "lost soul" of the little Black boys. In fact, it is ONLY him that can bring order out of this chaos. Black fathers have to step up and take their rightful position in The Universe.

This is an easy fix though; all Black fathers have to do is "stand on their square" and "git down for their crown". Fuck the mother and all her chicanery, spiteful ways, attempts to destroy and all the tricks and games she plays to get back at you. If she wants to go to court, fuck it!, go and show up and say what the fuck you gotta say Black Father. However, she wants to handle it, you meet her challenge head up. Do not give in one inch. The one thing you cannot not do is let the situation break you and quit.

Black on Black Crime

Chicago is out of control. There is a "Chicago" in damn near every Black community in America. In my opinion, the root cause of this is illuminated in the aforementioned subsection of "Black Fathers", as most of the violence is perpetrated by young Black boys or men. I rarely if ever hear of Black females being killed by other Black females in shootings. It's us. Black Men.

We are responsible for this. It is our fault. It is our problem, irrespective and regardless of whatever systematic oppression may or may not exist. It is our responsibility, irrespective and regardless of poverty, unemployment, poor schools or whatever the fuck. It don't fuckin' matter, this the game, this is the hand we were dealt and we have to play the muthaphucka. In my opinion, we should and can play a lot better than how we are playing.

I can go on and on and on and on and on and on about this, however, I'm going to conclude here and sum it up by sayin':

> it's weak to speak and blame somebody else...when you destroy yourself.......

Peace out
Sean G

Wednesday, March 14, 2018

Don't feel like writing much today, however, I always make at least 1 move toward my goals no matter how small or infinitesimal it may be. I make sure I do "something" each day toward my goal.

Went to the gym and got money, did my window cleaning route, ran some errands, bought a new camera and microphone to elevate my vlogging game. People seem to be enjoying my YouTube videos and I'm having fun doing them.

I am on a low carbohydrate, low sugar diet right now. Doing this will get me lean and eradicate my body fat. I'm upping my cardio game to compliment the diet to really get lean. I've increased my protein intake and upped my water consumption. I'm training at least 5 days a week at a minimum, but my goal is to train everyday to keep my mind, spirit and body in tune and intact. My health is my wealth. Yes, I will pass on to the next life at some point in the future, but I don't have to rush that process by eating fucked up foods, being sedentary, overweight, taking medications for illnesses I can cure on my own with diet change and exercise. And I can live a much more fuller and healthier life while I'm here by taking good care of my body, mind and soul.

Getting ready to go "down Souf" by my mother's house with Lil Sean in 2 weeks. He can't wait and neither can she. When them 2 get together it's "ova wit". I love the fact that they love each other the way that they do. It's an indescribable feeling.

I will be going to Atlanta to do my first ever book signing, and I will be appearing on Instinct Radio to talk about my book. I'm excited and looking forward to it. This book has taken on a life of it's own and I'm allowing it to live and do what it does.

Wednesday, March 21, 2018

I construct my plan then I work my plan to a muthaphuckin' T! I do not deviate one iota. I plan for contingencies and adjust and adapt accordingly when faced with unexpected events or happenings while in route to my destination, whatever that may be.

Everything is flowing smoothly, and I can see my progress. I have accomplished a lot in the last 26 months since walking out of federal prison (FCI Morgantown) and I am extremely pleased with my life. I have the dope life! My life is the shit! It's good to be me. Es Bueno Ser Yo!!!!

My book (aSTIGMAtism In My Soul – Volume I) is selling well and people seem to find it "interesting". That's the word I most often hear from those readers who have read it. They also mention that they love and respect my honesty, candor and forthrightness. The younger generation (millennials) like that it's "raw and hardcore". The youth always like and respect that real shit. The youth are always the ones who push the envelope and are open-minded to new things because they know no fear, have no concept of what fear is and aren't afraid to fail. Essentially, the younger generation doesn't give a fuck (they will try anything).

My YouTube channel is doing well and my subscriber numbers are growing every day. I really enjoy doing the videos. It's cool to see myself on a computer screen, ipad or cell phone. I have been getting some good feedback on my videos as well.

I continue to workout and exercise at least 7 days a week. I consistently eat clean foods and get my proper rest. I look good as a muthaphucka! I feel even better. My health is my wealth. My exercise, diet and rest is my "health insurance plan" and I pay my premium by working the fuck out, eating clean and sleeping. That's why I look so muthaphuckin' good!

I'm gone!

      Be True!

           Be Bold!

                Be Aggressive!

Sunday, March 25, 2018

Last night before I took it down (went to sleep), I did what I usually do every night when I get in the rack (bed), and that's to congratulate myself on "getting another inch" for that day. To go through everything that I accomplished that day that moved me "one inch" closer to my goals and destinations. "One inch at a time", that's how I measure my progress. No rush, no hurrying, no pressure, no monumental tasks, no crazy risks….. just one inch at a time. Just keep making progress Sean… just keep making progress Sean. That's what I tell myself.

What was interesting last night though was that I began to reflect and look at my current life and I was excited, happy and content with not knowing where my life was going and what was going to happen next or where I would end up in the short term. But I knew that as long as I kept living clean, doing the next right thing, staying positive, getting my inches, keep being the best me that I could be and not to "let up on my set up"; that if I did those things, that I would be fine. What I mean is that this book that I wrote and my YouTube channel are taking me places and introducing me to all kinds of people that I otherwise wouldn't have met had I not wrote my book. This part of my life is "up for grabs" and I have no idea where this book is going to take me but I know it will be a good place because I'm coming from my heart and soul with what I write.

So I was reflecting on that last night and it felt good. Then I took it down and got me 7.5 hours of great sleep so that I can keep looking as good as I do.

Peace

Tuesday, March 27, 2018

Peace! Good Morning! I'm up, energized, refreshed and ready to live this day as a Professional Life Liver! Stay focused on what's important, block out what's not important and move forward toward realizing my goals and dreams.

I am the only one who can stop me. I speak it so it is! I am having a lot of fun in my life right now. The uncertainty is exciting knowing that people are feeling my book and my YouTube videos and that sooner or later it will explode and reach a bunch of people and help some people to "git right".

Me and Lil Sean are getting ready to fly down to Georgia this Friday to spend time with my mother, his grandmother, and I'm going to be doing a radio show in Atlanta to promote the book and discuss some other topics. I'm also doing a book signing at Wings on Wheat in Stone Mountain. I'm sure to meet and see some people I haven't seen in a long time. I'm looking forward to it.

In this life "you have to go for what you know", "go for yours", "make shit happen". You can't sit back and wait for someone else to do something for you; you have to get the fuck up and go do that shit yourself if you want it done and done right! Life is what you make it.

Make your World what you want it to be!

Don't let up on your set-up!

Later that same day.........

Got my whole route done today, filed another motion for custody modification with family court to get full custody of My Sun. I am not jokin' or playin'. Picked Lil Sean up from school, came home and did 500 push-ups, made Lil Sean some dinner, got him a shower, got me a shower, did my stock market charts, uploaded some new video footage I shot today, checked Sean's homework and now I'm chillin' ready to take it down. Another successful day won.

There is not time for letting up on my preparations, moves and action plan. The time is now. Time is of the essence and not a single nanosecond can be wasted fuckin' around with bullshit. This is real and very serious. Yes, we do need time to unwind, relax and let loose in life, granted..... but when it's hustle time, it's muthaphuckin' HUSTLE TIME!!! All distractions must be eliminated, nuthin' ass niggaz in your life have to be removed, the self is put on the strictest discipline program of proper diet, exercise and rest. The mind must be calmed down as well as the spirit in order to reach a clarity that allows me to see the reality of my situation.

This is not a test. This is not a game. This is live and real. This is not a movie or comic strip. This is my life and it is real indeed. I must treat it as such.

I'm 49 years old and well on my way to "making my world what I want it to be."

Be True!   Be Bold!   Be Aggressive!

PRESS RELEASE   *Contact:* The Universe

For Immediate Release   *999.999.999 Pineal Gland Code*

MARCH 2018

THE UNITED STATES OF AMERICA DIAGNOSED WITH INTERNAL BLEEDING, MALIGNANT TUMORS AND CORROSIVE CANCER OF IT'S INTERNAL ORGANS!

The Sun, Milky Way Galaxy, The Universe – We are saddened to announce that the most powerful nation on the Planet Earth is ailing, suffering and dying from internal bleeding, malignant tumors and cancer. It's illnesses have long been discovered and thus far The United States of America has refused to seek treatment, medical attention and rehabilitation for its internal diseases.

The diagnosis is that The United States of America is suffering from:

1. The lack of justice for all of it's citizens
2. False representation and breach of Constitutional laws
3. Contempt, mistreatment and abuse of power in it's treatment of The Black American Male

We, The Universe, The Sun, Moon and Stars have carefully watched America's performance and continue to examine her actions and we are none to pleased with her treatment of our children, especially The Black American Male. The Black American Male belongs to us, The Universe, first and foremost and we love The Black American Male, as he is one of our most prized possessions and one of our greatest creations.

It seems that somehow America is lost on the fact that *"what you put out into The Universe, comes back to you with mathematical exactness. That what goes around ….. comes around."*

We, The Universe, The Sun, Moon and Stars will remind America that she is small potatoes in the overall scheme of things, as this Universe and everything in it belongs to us, The Sun, The Moon and The Stars.

The Prognosis

The United State of America is the #1 Super Power in the world today culturally, financially, and militarily. The United States of America has the #1 offensive military capabilities, weaponry and military defense mechanisms on the planet Earth. There are other nations in the world with similarly sophisticated military equipment as the United States, however, these nations do not want any smoke with America from a military perspective, as they know deep down in the recesses of their minds and souls that they cannot stand up to or withstand an "all out military offensive" from the United States of America.

The United States of America need not fear Vladimir Putin of Russia, Kim Jong Ung of North Korea, Xi Jinping of China nor Ram Nath Kovind of India nor any of their militaries. The United States need not fear any encroachment by any nation nor a foreign military invasion from any nation on the planet. All these bases are covered and the United States' Space Defense System in best in class.

However,.......................

The United States of America appears to be and will most likely destroy its own self from within. The United States of America has a disease and sickness that no other country on the planet has and this disease, if not treated quickly, will collapse all the major internal organs, veins and arteries of America. This disease which causes internal bleeding, tumors and ultimately terminal cancer is called "Racism" stemming from America's treatment of The Black American Male.

Yes, other countries do have caste systems and discriminate against each other internally, however, these countries are for the most part "homogeneous throughout" so it's not as cutting. Elite Russians discriminate against poverty-stricken Russians but they are "all still Russians". Chinese discriminate against other Chinese but they are "all still Chinese" at the end of the day. This is throughout the world from country to country so I will not belabor the point by pointing out each nation...you understand my point.

America is totally different and unique from the rest of the world. America has these citizens here that it captured 500 – 600 years ago through brutality, subjugation, degradation, torture, homicide, rape and force.

These citizens are of African descent and are known today as "Black Americans". America has since "so called freed" these citizens from physical captivity and bestowed upon them all of the civil rights, freedoms and liberties that all of its other inhabitants enjoy (even immigrants), however, it does so in words only.

In 2018, The United States of America is a bully. In 2018, The United State of America is the bully of the world playground and does not play by the rules.

You ask…. What rules do you speak of?

The rules I speak of are the ultimate rules. The only rules that cannot be bribed, circumvented or broken ever. These are the Universal Rules also known as "Universal Laws". America thumbs her nose up to The Universe and this is evident in her continued mistreatment of The Black American Male. It is common place in America to see Black American Males shot down and killed by agents of the United States Government's Military (white police officers) with impunity and no type of accountability or repercussions whatsoever.

It seems as though America deliberately allows this type of treatment to send some type of message to the Black American Male. But whether deliberate or coincidental, nonetheless the behavior of America persists and is left unchecked by America itself or society.

However, there is a Universal Law that says:

> "what you throw out into The Universe comes back to you
> With mathematical exactness."

> "what goes around comes around"

> "Karma"

I think the United States of America thinks she is exempt from this law. That due to her military might and financial clout that she can skirt Universal Laws. If this is the position of the United States of America, I think she is sadly mistaken and has made and continues to make a grave mistake.

No person, place or thing can escape "The All", "The Universe". No family, neighborhood, town, city, county, region, state or country can escape "The Universal Laws". NOBODY and NO THING!!!

Does America not know this? Does America not see that she, America, will cause her own demise? That all the other nations around the world (Russia, China, India) have to do is "sit back and watch America collapse from within".

You cannot treat people the way you do America and think The Sun, Moon and Stars in going to be OK with it. It doesn't work like that. You will pay The Universe what you owe for what you have done. EVERYBODY and EVERYTHING falls under this law.

America you have built up a balance and a debt so humungous with The Universe that man.... I don't know if you will be able to pay it off and stay intact. You are self-destructing America.

You best believe you will pay The Universe one day.

The Legacy We Leave

In my opinion, what we do at "this time" in "this life" will ring forward and forever for future posterity and generations to partake of and be proud or discard and be ashamed. I am a believer in "one's ability to free will, choice, judgement and reason" and therefore that we each and individually are responsible and have the ability to effect our own destiny, hence, we are able to dictate our legacy.

I know some who believe and subscribe to the notion and belief that "our lives have already been written and that we, in and of ourselves, are powerless to alter or change our destiny in any way shape or form". I for one am not of this opinion. For my contention is that if in fact this is true, then The Universe, God or The Supreme Being or whatever you believe or don't believe, has "favored" or "chosen" some to be better than others in whatever measure you want to choose.
I don't believe that The Universe would be so inclined to be prejudiced and selective in its creations. My feeling is that I, Sean X. Gunby Sr., have the ability to build and construct whatever life I want "I will for myself". I can "will" into existence anything that I want. It's my choices. It's my attitude. It's my belief. It's my self-confidence. It's my discipline. It's my concentration. It's my dedication. This will determine my legacy.

It's those defining moments of our lives that have a direct impact on our destiny. It's what we do when those defining moments present themselves. It's our response. It's our thoughts. It's our perspective. It's our planning. These and many more will determine our legacy that we leave.

I am in the process of leaving a legacy for Lil Sean's children's children can look to and draw strength and courage from. A reservoir of accomplishments, the overcoming of obstacles, the conquering of adversity and the confrontation of fears that they can read and drink from when they are thirsty for fortitude, determination and belief in themselves. I will leave this legacy. It is up to me and nobody else.

What will be your legacy that you leave?

+++

If you don't like what I wrote. Or. If you like what I wrote. I don't give a fuck!

--- Sean Xavier Gunby, Sr.

Made in the USA
Middletown, DE
05 September 2021